BETTY TALMADGE'S

LOVEJOY PLANTATION COOKBOOK

PEACHTREE PUBLISHERS, LTD.

Published by
PEACHTREE PUBLISHERS, LTD.
494 Armour Circle, N. E.
Atlanta, Georgia 30324

Copyright © 1983 Betty Talmadge

Design by Cindy McDaniel

Original Art by John Kollock

Library of Congress Catalog Number 83-61917

ISBN: 0-931948-44-4

10 9 8 7 6 5 4

CONTENTS

1 A MAGNOLIA SUPPER AT LOVEJOY   1

Belle Watling's Wicked Mint Julep • Tara Toasted Pecans • Sausage Minié Balls • Plantation Vegetables Relish Tray • Talmadge Country Ham • Southern Fried Chicken • Confederate Cucumber Mousse and Tomatoes • Scarlett's Carrots • True Grits à la Robert E. Lee • Rhett Butler's Biscuits • Aunt Pittypat's Homemade Peach Ice Cream • Lovejoy Lace Cookies • Fresh Iced Tea • Freshly Perked Coffee

2 BARBECUE ON THE LAWN OF THE PLANTATION   17

Beer in the Bucket • Roasted Suckling Pig • John Wilkes' Pit-Roasted Pig with Blazin' Barbecue Sauce • Twelve Oaks Brunswick Stew • Old South Cabbage Slaw • Crisp Atlanta Potatoes • Melanie's Marinated Cucumbers • Plumb Pickled Peaches • Dixie Breaking Bread • Mammy's Cracklin Cornbread • Southern Sweets from the Neighbors: Charlotte's Peanut Butter Pie • Virginia Callaway's Blueberry Pie • Tipsy Tom • Miss Ellen's Home-Brewed Iced Tea with Lemon Slices

3 A HONEYSUCKLE LUNCHEON AT TARA   37

Champagne Peach Punch • Garden Tomato Sandwiches on Cottage Dill Bread • Chick

*'n' Lily Salad • Cheese Wafers • Toasted
Sally Lunn Bread • Spicey Plums • Tipsy
Peaches • Miss Prissy's Sherried Fig Ice
Cream • Confederate Butter Balls • Petite
Pecan Tassies • Little Lady Lemon Pies •
Iced Coffee with Country Cream and
Brown Sugar*

4 THANKSGIVING, CHRISTMAS, AND   55
NEW YEAR'S AT LOVEJOY
*Celery Stalks • Stuffed Green Olives •
Cranberry Salad • Brandy-Baked
Thanksgiving Ham • Grandma Shingler's
Scalloped Oysters • Turnip Greens with
Fatback • City-Style Green Peas • Ocilla
Candied Sweet Potatoes • Refrigerator
Green Tomato Pickles • Criss-Cross Yeast
Rolls • Pumpkin-Pecan Pie • Angel Food
Cake with Ambrosia: Fruits of the Gods •
Charlotte Russe • Hot Coffee • Iced Tea*

*Company's Comin' Egg Nog • Nesselrode
Pudding • Louise Hastings' Fruitcake •
Christmas Coconut Cake • Miniature Ham
Biscuits with Sweet-Hot Mustard Sauce*

*Hot Pot Likker • Ringin'-in-the-New-Year
Relishes • Barbecued Spareribs • Blazin'
Barbecue Sauce • Black-Eyed Peas with Hog
Jowl • Greenback Collards • Rutabaga
Turnips • Tomato Marmalade • Green and
Red Pepper Jelly • Bentley's Homemade
Bran Bread • 'Cile's Corn Pones • Southern*

Gingerbread with Caramel Sauce • Coffee •
Hot Tea

5 KIDS, ANIMALS, GOOD TIMES,   89
AND GOOD FOOD
   Pigs on a Stick with Horseback Sauce •
   Hen Legs in Bean Beds • Ruff's Painted
   Hush Puppies • Back Yard Corn on the
   Cob • Rainbow Sugar Cookies • Billy T.
   Sherman's Chocolate Glutton Pie •
   Watermelon Slices • Ice Cream Cones •
   Gorp by Sam B. • Pink Lemonade •
   Strawberry Smoothies

6 TROTTERS, TALES, AND   101
OTHER WILD WEEDS
   Trotters, Pickled • Sawmill Chicken •
   Country Cracklins • Chitlins • Grandma
   Shingler's Liver Puddin' • Head Cheese
   Loaf • Liver Sausage • Mild Country Farm
   Sausage • Hot Country Farm Sausage •
   Jimmy's Brunswick Stew • Poke Salad
   Sambo • Poke Salit Helen • Hoecakes •
   Ferrol's Vegetable Garden Soup •
   Pomegranate Jelly • Old-Fashioned
   Quincedonia Preserves • Roast 'Possum

7 ME AND MARILYN MONROE—   123
MY MOVIE CAREER
   Country Fried Ham Biscuits with Red Eye
   Gravy • Catch-Up Egg Sandwich • Sausage
   Pinwheels • Deviled Eggs with Bacon •
   Traveling Grits • Chocolate Waffle

Sandwiches with Strawberry Cream Cheese
• Just Grab an Apple • Fruit on a Stick •
Brenda's Breakfast Burritos • Cold
Coca-Cola • Cold Orange Juice • Hot Coffee
• Hot Chocolate

8 THE POLITICS OF FINE FOOD   135
Old Crow on Ice • Sacked Wine • Lame
Duck Pâté on Ceded Wafers • Baloney •
Crow Balls • Dark Horse Dip and Bitters •
Beat Salad • Waterloo Celery with Old
Goat Cheese • Sour Grapes Salad • Cooked
Goose in Whipped Potato Cups • Depressed
Duck • Agony of deFeet • Ill Wind Beans •
Stewed Tomatoes • Beaten Biscuits • Hat in
the Ring Cake • Bar the Nuts

Doves with Gravy on Thick Toast • Capitol
Quail • Wild Rice • Orator's Onions in
Foil • Corn Sticks • Senate Salad with
House Dressing • Baked Apples • Fried Up
Okra • Greenhorn Beans with Small
Potatoes • Filibuster Pie • Coffee with
Cream and Sugar

INDEX   160

A MAGNOLIA SUPPER AT LOVEJOY

Welcome to Lovejoy Plantation.

Come in and make yourself at home. Supper will be ready soon, so have a seat and let's talk a little. I want to tell you about this house.

I love this old plantation. A lot of precious memories — many happy ones and a few sad ones — have been invested in this house since we moved here in 1946. Sometimes I feel I'm really more of a friend than an owner.

And sometimes I have a feeling that the house itself is alive — from those hand-hewn timbers on the wall to the stately white columns. Every house has a story to tell, you know, and I suppose this one has more stories than most. After a century and a half, it ought to.

It was already an "old" house when the Civil War broke out; it had been built in 1836. A mighty enemy army came marching through this part of the country, burning and looting, but the house escaped somehow. There's plenty of history here. Those columns out front, for instance, are hollow inside. They say grain was stored in them during the War to keep it from marauding Yankee soldiers. And in a grove of trees right down the road, some men were digging a year or two back and unearthed Minié balls, utensils, uniform buttons, and other artifacts from that period.

You're right in the heart of *Gone With the Wind* country, you know. This very house, according to local

1

Sometimes I have a feeling that the house itself is alive

historians, was probably Margaret Mitchell's inspiration for Twelve Oaks, the family home of Scarlett O'Hara's beloved Ashley Wilkes.

And that old house just across the field there — the one you can see from the front porch — is supposed to be the inspiration for Tara.

It used to be called the Fitzgerald Place, and it belonged to Margaret Mitchell's mother's family. Miss Mitchell visited there many times when she was a girl, and it was in that house that she heard many of the rich family legends that she incorporated into her great book.

It was built by her great-grandfather, Philip Fitzgerald, who immigrated to Georgia from County Tipperary in 1825. He was supposedly Miss Mitchell's model for Scarlett's blustery Irish-born father, Gerald O'Hara. Both, incidentally, were strong Catholics.

The Fitzgerald Place was originally located about four miles from here — the next plantation up the road. I bought it several years ago when it was about to be torn down and had it moved here. I hope I'm able to have it renovated someday.

Oh, I know you were expecting Tara to be much grander than that. You envisioned massive columns and a sweeping veranda, like the Tara in the movie, didn't you? Well, if you read the book carefully, you'll find that "clumsy sprawling building" right out there was what Miss Mitchell had in mind for her Tara.

That's Hollywood for you.

But I don't think you have to settle for just one version of Tara. I bought the movie-set facade of the plantation a few years ago from a man who had kept it stored for years in an old barn. (The story of how I found it way out in the country on the other side of Atlanta is a

3

Many Civil War artifacts have been found on the plantation

true tragicomedy and would almost make a book in itself. More about that later.)

It's my great dream someday to put that facade up and unite the reality with the myth. Can't you just picture it out there under that huge old oak tree? Can't you just see Scarlett and Rhett strolling under the magnolias and Ashley and Melanie sipping tall, cool drinks on the veranda?

My dream is to have Twelve Oaks and Tara here in the land where they belong and where they were spawned in Peggy Mitchell's wonderful imagination.

As you can tell, I am in love — like a few million other people all over the world — with *Gone With the Wind*. I love both the Hollywood dream-castle myth and the solid Georgia-clay reality. I think both should have a place in our hearts. The South of the storybooks is the South that the tourists expect to see. And who can blame them? The "other" South, the real one that we native Southerners know and love so well, is here, too.

The Southern tradition, however you look at it, is alive and well at Lovejoy Plantation.

And "having company" — cooking and serving and entertaining guests — is as much a part of the Southern tradition as Spanish moss and white columns and magnolia trees are.

People who lived on plantations way out in the country like this just naturally loved having friends and kinfolks visit for a spell. This is how the legendary "Southern hospitality" was born.

Here at Lovejoy Plantation, where Southern hospitality has reigned since the 1830s, it is a way of life. Love, laughter, memories, good friends and good food.

Speaking of good food, I think our Magnolia Supper is on the table. Let's go in.

A Magnolia Supper at Lovejoy

(for Yankees and other tourists)

Belle Watling's Wicked Mint Julep
Tara Toasted Pecans
Sausage Minié Balls
Plantation Vegetables Relish Tray
Talmadge Country Ham
Southern Fried Chicken
Confederate Cucumber Mousse and Tomatoes
Scarlett's Carrots
True Grits à la Robert E. Lee
Rhett Butler's Biscuits
Aunt Pittypat's Homemade Peach Ice Cream
Lovejoy Lace Cookies
Fresh Iced Tea
Freshly Perked Coffee

BELLE WATLING'S WICKED MINT JULEP

Ingredients
for each drink:

leaves from 2 long mint sprigs
1 tsp. sugar
splash of water
3 oz. bourbon
finely cracked ice
2 long mint sprigs

Directions:

Muddle mint leaves and sugar in glass. Add water and bourbon. Strain, pouring mixture into a small glass filled with ice. Stir until glass frosts. Top with mint sprigs.

TARA TOASTED PECANS

Ingedients:

1 quart fine quality pecan halves
½ cup butter, melted
salt

Directions:

Preheat oven to 250°. Spread pecans evenly on large baking sheet. Drizzle with butter. Bake 1 hour, stirring occasionally. Remove from oven. Salt pecans while hot. Store in airtight container.

SAUSAGE MINIÉ BALLS

Ingredients
for 30 balls:

1 lb. hot sausage
2 cups sharp Cheddar cheese, finely grated
3 cups biscuit mix

Directions:

Mix all ingredients. Pinch off bits and make 1-inch balls. Bake at 425° for 10-12 minutes. Serve hot.

PLANTATION VEGETABLES RELISH TRAY

Ingredients
for 8-10 servings:

½ head cauliflower
4 stalks broccoli
1 large onion
12-16 mushrooms
4 stalks celery
1 large can pitted black olives
1 bottle Italian dressing
1 package dry Italian dressing mix
parsley
endive

Directions:

Cut fresh vegetables into bite-sized pieces. Drain olives. Put all ingredients in plastic bowl with airtight cover. Shake gently. Refrigerate overnight. Shake occasionally to mix vegetables with marinade. Drain. Arrange on

8

serving tray. Garnish with parsley and endive.

TALMADGE COUNTRY HAM

Ingredients:

1 country-cured ham (dry salt
  cured)
water to soak in
water to cook in
6 onions
2 cups brown sugar
2 cups vinegar
2 bay leaves
24 cloves
Glaze:
1 cup brown sugar
1 tsp. dry mustard

Directions:

Soak ham overnight in water.
Drain. Place ham in large, heavy
pan on top of stove. Cover with
water and remaining ingredients
(except glaze). Simmer about 20
minutes per lb. Cool in liquid.
Remove skin and excess fat.

Make glaze: Mix brown sugar
and mustard. Spread over top of
ham. Bake 20 minutes at 450°.

Slice and serve.

Talmadge Tip:

Allow 1½ oz. cooked ham per
person. This style ham is *very*
rich.

SOUTHERN FRIED CHICKEN

Ingredients:

chicken parts
salt water
buttermilk
flour
pepper
lard

Directions:

Place chicken parts in salt water. Refrigerate 2-3 hours or overnight. Drain. Dip in buttermilk. Roll pieces in flour. Sprinkle with pepper. Heat lard in heavy skillet (lard should be about 2 inches deep) until it just begins to smoke. Add chicken pieces. Do not crowd. Cover. Fry 15 minutes. Turn and brown other side about 15 minutes. Drain in colander lined with paper towels.

Talmadge Tip:

Listen to the grease to know to turn the chicken. When it sounds like water is being added and makes popping noises, it is ready to turn.

10

CONFEDERATE CUCUMBER MOUSSE AND TOMATOES

Ingredients
for 12 servings:
5 large cucumbers
2 cups ginger ale
2 packages lime gelatin
2 envelopes plain gelatin
Tabasco sauce, heavy dash
1 Tbl. sugar
1 cup sour cream
1 cup mayonnaise
lettuce and tomatoes for garnish

Directions:
Peel and grate cucumbers. Drain one hour. Heat half the ginger ale. Dissolve all gelatin. Cool. Mix in remaining ingredients (except garnish). Pour into fancy mold. Chill until set. Unmold on layer of lettuce and sliced tomatoes.

Talmadge Tip:
The dash of Tabasco sauce gives this extra zip.

11

SCARLETT'S CARROTS

Ingredients:

1 lb. carrots, very coarsely grated
½ cup butter
¼ cup brown sugar
¼ cup Wild Turkey liqueur

Directions:

Sauté carrots in butter. Add brown sugar. Stir until melted. Add liqueur. Serve hot.

Talmadge Tip:

Be sure the carrots are grated, not sliced. A food processor works well.

TRUE GRITS À LA ROBERT E. LEE

*Ingredients
for 6-8 servings:*

4 cups water
2 tsp. salt
1 cup grits, plain or speckled
2 cups sharp Cheddar cheese, grated
¼ cup butter
½ tsp. Worcestershire sauce
4 eggs, separated

Directions:

Bring salted walter to a boil. Add grits. Cook until thick. Add 1½ cups of the cheese and all of the butter and Worcestershire sauce. Remove from heat. Beat in

12

egg yolk. (Add milk, if necessary, to make them medium-thick.) Beat egg whites until stiff. Fold into grits. Pour into greased 1½-quart casserole. Top with remaining ½ cup cheese. Bake at 350° for 35 minutes.

RHETT BUTLER'S BISCUITS

Ingredients:

5 cups self-rising flour
⅓ cup sugar
1 cup shortening
2 packages yeast, dissolved in ¼ cup lukewarn water
2 cups buttermilk
butter, melted

Directions:

Sift dry ingredients. Cut in shortening. Add yeast and buttermilk. Mix well. Chill 1 hour. Roll and cut. Set aside to rise 1 hour in warm place. Bake at 350° for 15 minutes. Brush with melted butter as biscuits start to brown. Continue to bake until brown.

Talmadge Tip:

These can be made and refrigerated up to 10 days ahead.

AUNT PITTYPAT'S HOMEMADE PEACH ICE CREAM

Ingredients:

2 cups sugar
2 Tbl. flour
4 eggs, slightly beaten
2 cups half-and-half
2 cans undiluted evaporated milk
12 overripe peaches, peeled, crushed, and sweetened with 1 cup sugar

Directions:

Mix sugar and flour. Add eggs and half-and-half. Cook in double boiler, stirring constantly, until mixture steams. Remove from heat. Add evaporated milk. Pour into ice cream freezer. When mixture reaches mushy consistency, add peaches. Continue freezing until firm. To serve, place scoops of ice cream in large bowl. Let guests help themselves.

LOVEJOY LACE COOKIES

Ingredients:

2¼ cups old-fashioned oatmeal
2¼ cups light brown sugar
3 Tbl. flour
1 tsp. salt
1 cup butter, melted

1 egg, slightly beaten
1 tsp. vanilla

Directions: Mix dry ingredients by hand. Add remaining ingredients. Mix well. Drop onto greased cookie sheet. Dough should be about quarter-sized pieces. Bake 8-10 minutes at 350°.

BARBECUE ON THE LAWN OF THE PLANTATION

When my guests drive through Lovejoy Plantation, they see a piece of the Old South that seems unchanged by time. The setting of old oaks and magnolias, the mighty antebellum columns, and the stillness of one thousand acres of countryside pulls them into the storybook South.

That happened to me the first time I came here almost forty years ago. But I can assure you, Lovejoy Plantation was not then as you see it today. It was a run-down old house with no plumbing or electricity, surrounded by weeds and broomsage. Still, I was so excited over the prospect of restoring this place, I couldn't stand it. "Miss Ada" Healey (Mrs. William T. Healey, Sr.) had become a good friend that I really leaned on in those days, and I couldn't wait for her to see this hundred- and-ten-year-old treasure I wanted to turn into a home.

"Hasn't it got possibilities?" I asked as she scanned the overgrown house that included only one closet.

"Yes, Honey. For spending lots of money," she answered dryly. And she was right. I've been spending money on this house ever since.

At one point, we almost gave up the idea because people kept telling us the house was too old and too far gone. But we finally found an architect who said he

17

The house's original grandeur has been lovingly restored

could do the job. We spent $12,000 to get the house livable — with indoor plumbing and electricity. That was a chunk of money in 1946, but even then, I really had only two rooms finished — my bedroom and, of course, my kitchen.

We were a long way from the house-warming stage when my former husband told me that he wanted to have Red and Ralph McGill (editor of the *Atlanta Constitution*) out for dinner. I looked around the room a little horrified and said, "We don't even have a table big enough to seat Red and Ralph McGill and the four of us." That's how I got my first breakfast room table. I went to Rich's the next day and bought it for that dinner. I eventually got a dining room table and finished all the rooms in the house. But every time I look around, there

18

is a new project that needs to be done. When I get it propped up over here, it falls down over there.

The expense of caring for an antebellum home became the motivation for a business I started about three years ago. I realized this house was a lifetime project and that if I planned to keep it the way it should be kept, I had to find a new source of money. Opening my house for tours and special parties seemed to be the perfect answer. I had the right setting for Southern hospitality, and I've certainly given plenty of parties during my many years as a politician's wife.

I find that the business of entertaining is usually more fun than work. My greatest challenge is not making the food or the garnishes perfect — down-home food doesn't have to be fussy — but making sure my guests have a good time.

I learned a long time ago — when I was 24 years old and First Lady of Georgia — not to get nervous over a party. At that tender young age, I found myself faced with a guest list of 400 people — the entire Georgia Legislature and their spouses — for a dinner party the next night. When you've got one day to prepare dinner for that many folks, you don't have time to be nervous. You have to become organized and resourceful very quickly. Remember, there were no rental businesses in those days; I had to borrow everything.

I rounded up my friends and we threw hams and turkeys into the oven like there was no tomorrow. And it turned out there wasn't. The party had to be postponed until the following week because of a conflict with the Legislature's schedule.

I shifted from high gear into low and learned a second lesson — how to be flexible. If Plan A doesn't

Art Buchwald enjoyed playing the role of Rhett Butler

Barbecue on the lawn is a Southern, summer tradition

20

work, put Plan B into effect, and remember that making people feel at home is the bottom line for a successful party.

One way I accomplish this is to add simple touches that make my guests feel special. I have found that when people visit Lovejoy Plantation, they feel as though they are stepping into the fantasy world of Scarlett and Rhett. They imagine this is Twelve Oaks and they've come to visit Ashley Wilkes. I try to add to that mystique.

When Art Buchwald came to Atlanta a couple of years ago to attend the American Booksellers Association convention, his publishers hired me to arrange a party in honor of his book *Laid Back in Washington*. I took the *Gone With the Wind* movie poster of Clark Gable embracing Vivian Leigh and superimposed a photo of Art — grinning and smoking a cigar — over Gable. Not exactly *Gone With the Wind* but definitely *Laid Back in Washington*. Art loved it so much I had to send him a copy for his living room.

When Phyllis Diller came here for a Magnolia Supper, I gave her a poster with her picture in Miss Leigh's spot. She didn't exactly look like Scarlett in her white boots and white plastic mini-dress, but she loved playing the part. Everybody wants to be Scarlett or Rhett.

I also amuse my guests by naming dishes after them. Scarlett's carrots (from the Magnolia Supper) were recently named Jerome Holland's Carrots in honor of the ambassador who came to Lovejoy Plantation for the American Red Cross Board of Governors dinner.

I hope I make my guests comfortable, because I'm always comfortable when I'm entertaining. I try to plan things well ahead, and I almost always stick to my

Magnolia Supper or Magnolia Barbecue when I cater a party, because I know these menus well.

The barbecue is a big hit because it's fun and because there is something wonderful about being out in the country and smelling pork roasting over hickory coals.

Remember . . . Scarlett smelled those hickory logs burning long before she reached Twelve Oaks for one of John Wilkes' famous barbecues.

Lovejoy Plantation
Magnolia Barbecue

(for our foreign friends and the local gentry)

Beer in the Bucket

Roasted Suckling Pig

*John Wilkes' Pit-Roasted Pig
with Blazin' Barbecue Sauce*

Twelve Oaks Brunswick Stew

Old South Cabbage Slaw

Crisp Atlanta Potatoes

Melanie's Marinated Cucumbers

Plumb Pickled Peaches

Dixie Breaking Bread

Mammy's Cracklin Cornbread

Southern Sweets from the Neighbors:

Charlotte's Peanut Butter Pie

Virginia Callaway's Blueberry Pie

Tipsy Tom

*Miss Ellen's Home-Brewed Iced Tea
with Lemon Slices*

BEER IN THE BUCKET

Ingredients: large galvanized washbucket or
    tub
    cracked ice
    canned or bottled beer

Directions: Fill tub half full with ice. Lay on beer cans. Cover with ice. Let guests help themselves.

ROASTED SUCKLING PIG

Ingredients: 20-40 lb. pig, dressed by butcher
    ½ gallon lemon juice
    1 head fresh garlic (8-10 cloves),
    minced
    1 cup salt
    clean rocks

Directions: Marinate pig in lemon juice and garlic overnight. Remove from marinade. Rub pig with salt. Put rocks inside body cavity to retain shape of pig's body. Put rocks in pig's mouth, so apple will fit there later. Close cavity with wire. Insert thermometer into flesh. Do not let it touch bone. Place pig on hot grill over hickory coals (about 200°-250°). Puncture skin several times with sharp knife. After 1 hour, cover ears and tail with damp cloths. Keep cloths damp as pig cooks, to keep them from burning. Continue cooking 12-14 hours, or until internal temperature reaches 170°. To serve, remove pig from grill to large wooden slab. Remove rock from mouth. Insert apple. Use jumbo olives for eyes.

Talmadge Tip:

Use this small pig as an edible table decoration. The large, pit-roasted one will be the primary "eating" pig for a large party.

JOHN WILKES' PIT-ROASTED PIG

Ingredients for 100
to 120 servings:

1 100-lb pig, dressed weight
shovel
pit
hickory wood
bed springs
4 metal garbage can lids
iron pot or bucket
large spoon
2 quarts water
½ cup salt
1 tsp. red pepper
1 tsp. black pepper
1 cup vinegar

Directions: First, locate a pig. About three weeks ahead, call a local butcher or supermarket to place the order. The whole hog is festive and decorative, but fresh hams or pork shoulders cook more efficiently. They are more economical than ribs. Have the butcher remove the head and knuckles, and saw pig's backbone to lay spread-eagle while roasting. In the meantime, dig the pit on solid ground. It should be about twelve inches to sixteen inches deep, three and a half feet wide, and five feet long. Slope and taper the pit on either end.

Fill the pit with one or two bushels of oak or hickory twigs. Burn down to ashes. This dries out the pit.

Make a second fire near one end of the pit. This will supply the coals to cook the meat during the night-and-day-long roasting time. Spread them conservatively as needed for a slow fire under the meat. Lay iron rods, bunk bed springs, or heavy hog wire mesh over the pit to support the pig. Lay the whole pig on this rack, spread-eagled, meat side down.

Toast the pig with a mint julep. Wish him good luck and thank him for what he is about to do for you.

Make heavy brine with remaining ingredients. Turn and baste meat during cooking. Roast slowly 12 to 18 hours, or until internal temperature is 170°. Blazin' Barbecue Sauce is added after the pig is cooked. It will burn, if applied during roasting. The brine permeates and seasons the roasting meat.

If you add too many coals, the dripping grease will catch fire and flare up. Smother these flames with the back of the shovel.

After the pig is properly blessed and cooking, cover with four clean, metal garbage can lids or a metal roofing sheet (old Coca-Cola signs have also been used). This retains the heat during the early morning hours, but it's loose enough to let smoke circulate slowly and season the meat.

The last eight to ten hours of cooking, turn pig over, skin side down. This will render the fat out of the skin while cooking. As the fat accumulates around ribs and shoulders, collect it with the large spoon. Save it in the iron pot. It congeals into lard. Remember: cook slowly to retain moisture and prevent burning. Use no barbecue sauce during cooking.

When the pig is done, slice and/or chop meat and serve with Blazin' Barbecue Sauce.

Talmadge Tip: After the long night, when you turn the pig, pick off little bits and pieces of pork. These make a great breakfast with hot coffee.

BLAZIN' BARBECUE SAUCE

Ingredients:

1¼ cup catsup
⅔ cup oil
1 cup vinegar
5 Tbl. Worcestershire sauce
½ cup brown sugar
¼ cup water
2 Tbl. dry mustard
3 tsp. freshly grated ginger
1 clove garlic, minced
1 lemon, thinly sliced
3 Tbl. butter
heavy dash Tabasco sauce
salt
pepper

Directions:

Mix and simmer all ingredients in pot on top of stove. Pour on barbecued pork — *after* the pork has finished cooking.

Talmadge Tip:

The sugar in the sauce will cause it to burn, if applied during long cooking. This sauce can be made 2 or 3 days ahead.

TWELVE OAKS BRUNSWICK STEW

Ingredients
for 50 servings:

3 hens, 5 lbs. each
1 hog's head
1 large bottle catsup
4 lbs. okra
2 gallons canned tomatoes
2 onions, grated
5 unpeeled lemons, cut into pieces
2 Tbl. sugar
2 Tbl. Tabasco sauce
½ cup apple cider vinegar
3 Tbl. Worcestershire sauce
1 gallon white cream-style corn

Directions:

Boil hens in water to cover. Save broth. Bone and cut hens into serving-sized pieces. Boil and bone hog's head. Drain, discarding broth. Mix all ingredients except corn. Cook one hour and then add corn. Simmer until thick and rich.

Talmadge Tip:

This is what we cook inside on the kitchen stove for the crowd. We keep it hot outside in the old iron washpot over a wood fire.

29

OLD SOUTH CABBAGE SLAW

Ingredients
for 20 servings:

1 cup corn oil
1 cup sugar
1 cup apple cider vinegar
2 tsp. celery seed
2 tsp. dry mustard
salt
pepper
1 large cabbage, coarsely shredded
1 large onion, sliced in rings
2 green peppers, coarsely chopped

Directions:

Combine oil, sugar, and vinegar. Boil slowly for 5 minutes. Add celery seed, mustard, salt, and pepper. Cool slightly. Combine cabbage, onions, and peppers with marinade in bowl. Chill 24 hours.

CRISP ATLANTA POTATOES

Ingredients:

new potatoes, unpeeled
vegetable oil, 1½ inches deep
salt

Directions:

Scrub potatoes. Cut paper-thin, leaving skin on. Fill skillet 1½ inches deep with oil. Heat until hot, but not smoking. Drop in slices one at a time. Do not crowd. When light brown, turn and brown other side. Remove and drain. Salt to taste. Serve hot or cold.

MELANIE'S MARINATED CUCUMBERS

Ingredients for 50 servings:

1 gallon unpeeled cucumbers, thinly sliced
8 small onions, thinly sliced
2 green peppers, finely chopped
ice
½ cup salt
Marinade:
5 cups vinegar
5 cups sugar
1½ tsp. turmeric
1½ tsp. ground cloves
1½ tsp. mustard seed
2 tsp. celery seed

Directions:

Layer vegetables, salt, and ice in jars or large crock. Let set 3 hours. Drain. Boil marinade ingredients. Pour over drained vegetables. Refrigerate. Serve cold.

PLUMB PICKLED PEACHES

Ingredients: 4 lbs. small peaches, ripe but firm
1 Tbl. whole cloves
1 stick cinnamon
1 lb. sugar
2 cups vinegar

Directions: Wash and peel peaches. Cook slowly with remaining ingredients until tender, but not broken. Chill in syrup. Refrigerate until ready to serve.

DIXIE BREAKING BREAD

Ingredients: store-bought barbecue bread (soft, white bread with individual portions baked together) butter, melted

Directions: Pour butter over bread. Bake at 400° until hot and crispy. Let guests pull off their own hot, buttery slabs.

32

MAMMY'S CRACKLIN CORNBREAD

Ingredients:

4 cups buttermilk
4 cups cornmeal
⅔ cup flour
⅔ cup sugar
1 tsp. soda
1 Tbl. salt
2 eggs
2 cups cracklins, finely chopped

Directions:

Sift dry ingredients together. Beat eggs with buttermilk. Mix all ingredients. Pour into well-greased and papered loaf pans. Bake at 400° for 1 hour, or until done. Slice and serve with country butter.

CHARLOTTE'S PEANUT BUTTER PIE

Ingredients
for 6 to 8 servings:

1 cup confectioners' sugar
½ cup crunchy peanut butter
1 pie shell, baked
Filling:
⅔ cup sugar
¼ cup cornstarch
¼ tsp. salt
2 cups milk, scalded
2 Tbl. butter
3 egg yolks, beaten
1 tsp. vanilla
Meringue:
3 egg whites
⅛ tsp. cream of tartar
3 Tbl. sugar

Directions:

Blend peanut butter and confectioners' sugar. Spread all but 3 Tbl. on bottom of pie shell. Save remainder for topping.

Make filling: Blend sugar, corn starch, and salt. Slowly add scalded milk. Place over medium heat. Cook, stirring constantly. Slowly add yolks and butter. Continue stirring until thickened. Set aside and stir in vanilla. Pour over peanut butter mixture.

Make meringue: Beat egg whites, sugar, and cream of tartar

until fluffy. Spread over filling. Top meringue with the remaining peanut butter mixture. Place in 300° oven until meringue is lightly browned. Serve at room temperature or chilled.

VIRGINIA CALLAWAY'S BLUEBERRY PIE

Ingredients:

1 cup water
1 cup sugar
1 cup blueberries, canned or fresh
2 Tbl. cornstarch
4 cups fresh blueberries
1 baked pie shell
whipped cream

Directions:

Boil water, sugar, and 1 cup blueberries 10 minutes. Strain. Dissolve cornstarch in cold water. Add to blueberry mixture. Cook until thick. Cool. Add 4 cups fresh blueberries. Put in pie shell. Top with whipped cream.

Talmadge Tip:

I also like to serve this with whipped cream *and* ice cream. It is super.

TIPSY TOM

Ingredients:
ladyfingers
blackberry wine
boiled vanilla custard
sliced almonds
muscat raisins
whipped cream

Directions:
Line bottom and sides of large glass bowl with ladyfingers. Soak with wine. Layer custard, almonds, and raisins. Refrigerate overnight. Top with whipped cream to serve.

Talmadge Tip:
This recipe has no exact proportions. Just put it together according to how much of each ingredient you like.

A HONEYSUCKLE LUNCHEON AT TARA

How would you like to come to a luncheon on the veranda of Tara? The honeysuckle is blooming and it's a beautiful day for having a crunchy chicken salad outside.

All you'll need to bring is your imagination. Pretend we're sashaying under the magnolia trees with Scarlett and Rhett while I tell you how "Tara" became a part of Lovejoy plantation.

Some years ago, I tried to buy the old Fitzgerald place from a man who lived out of state. But he was renting the house to a family at the time, and wasn't interested in selling.

I kept thinking how wonderful it would be to put together a *Gone With the Wind* museum complex with the house Margaret Mitchell supposedly had in mind when she created Tara, and the one Hollywood designed for the movie. But at that point, thinking was all I could do.

Then in the fall of 1979, I saw an article in the *Atlanta Constitution* that rekindled my dream. I learned that the Tara movie facade was still stored in a warehouse somewhere outside Atlanta. I looked up the man who owned it — a businessman named Julian M. Foster — and asked if he would consider selling it.

I was shocked when Mr. Foster said $175,000 was his asking price. The Tara set cost $250,000 to build in 1939, so in that sense, Mr. Foster's price sounded like a bargain. But I certainly wasn't able to pay that for it.

The old Fitzgerald place may have been the inspiration for Tara

Even when he came down to $75,000 a few weeks later, I had to say no. But I wanted to have a look at it anyway. Mr. Foster agreed to take me to see it, but he was so concerned about revealing the location, he practically blindfolded me. After a lot of driving around, we finally arrived at a "hog parlor" barn near Alpharetta, and I got to look at what amounted to a pile of old lumber.

I didn't have any idea what it was worth. It didn't look very valuable in that condition.

As it turned out, I bargained with Mr. Foster all the way from $175,000 down to $5,000. During the time we were negotiating, he received notice from the owner of the hog parlor that he would have to move Tara. He didn't want to go to that expense, so he accepted my

$5,000 offer, and I began to make plans to have it moved.

Unfortunately, Mr. Foster died before we completed the transaction, and once again, I almost gave up on my dream of owning the Tara set. He had been so secretive about where the barn was located that I couldn't find it. I drove around Alpharetta for days looking for it and finally hired a pilot to take me up in an airplane. Still I couldn't find it.

I finally called Mrs. Foster and said, "I can't spend the rest of my life looking for Tara. Surely there's got to be a cancelled check somewhere with the barn owner's name on it." She finally found one of Mr. Foster's rent checks with the man's name on it. I looked him up in the phone book and called him to explain what I wanted. He had no idea what he had been storing all that time.

I got directions to the barn, and found out I had been only three miles from it during my search. After restoration architect Norman Askins certified the authenticity of the Tara set, I had it moved to a safe place. Six months later, my dream moved another step closer to reality.

The old Fitzgerald place suddenly became available. The house had been vacant for a while and vandals were stripping out the mantels and woodwork. I called the owner on the phone to let him know about it, and within thirty minutes, I had bought the place for $1,000. That was only the beginning of the expense, however, because I had to have it dismantled and moved.

I went to look at the house as soon as I bought it, and vandals had taken all the doors down and stacked them up. I guess they were planning to come back for them. I took those doors with me that night. I wasn't about to let them get away.

The house looks kind of sad right now without its porch. I don't know how, but I hope to be able to attach the movie facade to the old house. If it can be done, I'll have the honeysuckle luncheon on the veranda, and then we'll go into the parlor for mint juleps.

Honeysuckle Luncheon at Tara

(for ladies only)

Champagne Peach Punch
Garden Tomato Sandwiches on
Cottage Dill Bread
Chick 'n' Lily Salad
Cheese Wafers
Toasted Sally Lunn Bread
Spicey Plums   Tipsy Peaches
Miss Prissy's Sherried Fig Ice Cream
Confederate Butter Balls
Petite Pecan Tassies
Little Lady Lemon Pies
Iced Coffee with Country Cream
and Brown Sugar

CHAMPAGNE PEACH PUNCH

Ingredients:

1 can peaches, undrained
3 sprigs fresh mint, leaves only
3 Tbl. lime juice
⅓ cup orange juice
⅛ tsp. lime rind, grated
⅛ tsp. orange rind, grated
1 quart chilled ginger ale
champagne, to taste
mint for garnish

Directions:

Whirl peaches and juice in blender to purée. Add mint, juices, and rinds. Chill. Just before serving, add ginger ale and champagne. Garnish with mint sprigs.

GARDEN TOMATO SANDWICHES

*Ingredients
for each sandwich:*

garden-fresh tomatoes
bacon strips, fried
Vidalia onion, thinly sliced
fresh lettuce
salt
pepper
mayonnaise
tiny slices of Cottage Dill Bread

Directions:

Arrange ingredients on trays.

Let guests make their own sandwiches as appetizers while sipping Champagne Peach Punch.

Talmadge Tip: My friend Jim Wood originated
this recipe.

COTTAGE DILL BREAD

Ingredients
for 2 loaves (6-by-3-
by-2½-inch pans):

¼ cup warm milk (105°-115°)
1 envelope dry yeast
1 Tbl. sugar
1 cup creamed cottage cheese
2 Tbl. onion, coarsely chopped
2 Tbl. butter
1 egg
1 tsp. salt
2¼ cups flour
¼ cup wheat germ
1 Tbl. dried dill
oil
1 egg
1 Tbl. water

Directions:

Put milk, yeast, and sugar in blender. Stir. Let stand 5 minutes. Process 10 seconds. Add cheese, onion, butter, and egg. Process 20 seconds.

In mixing bowl, combine dry ingredients. Add cottage cheese mixture. Stir with wooden spoon until dough pulls away from sides of bowl. Turn out onto floured surface and knead about 5 minutes.

Brush dough with oil and place in large bowl. Cover. Let rise in warm place until doubled in size (about 1¼ hours). Punch down.

Divide and place in 2 6-by-3-by-2½-inch loaf pans. Let rise until doubled.

Beat eggs with water. Brush tops of loaves to glaze.

Bake at 350° until browned.

Talmadge Tip:

Jimmy Bentley makes this himself.

CHICK 'N' LILY SALAD

Ingredients:

4 cups cooked chicken, diced
2 cups white seedless grapes
5 stalks celery, finely chopped
1 cup mayonnaise
2 Tbl. vinegar
½ tsp. celery salt
¼ tsp. turmeric powder
¼ tsp. dry mustard
1 Tbl. sugar
½ cup sliced almonds, toasted
salt
pepper
5 cantaloupes, chilled

Directions:

Mix and chill ingredients for salad, saving almonds for garnish. To make lilies, cut cantaloupes in halves, using a zig-zag pattern. To make petals, use a small knife. Peel back 1 layer of rind, then 1 layer of inside green. Fill lilies with salad. Garnish with almonds.

Talmadge Tip:

I call this one layer of rind, one layer of green, and one layer of good.

CHEESE WAFERS

Ingredients:

1 lb. sharp Cheddar cheese, grated
2 cups butter
3¼-3½ cups flour
red pepper

Directions:

Cream cheese and butter. Add remaining ingredients. Put in a cookie press with a cheese straw blade. Force onto cookie sheet in 1-inch wafers. Bake at 375° 10-15 minutes. Do not brown.

TOASTED SALLY LUNN BREAD

Ingredients:

1 cup lard
½ cup sugar
1 cup boiling water
2 yeast cakes
1 cup lukewarm water
2 eggs
6 cups flour
1 tsp. baking powder
1 tsp. baking soda
1 tsp. salt
butter for baking and toasting

Directions:

Cream lard with sugar. Add boiling water. Cool. Dissolve yeast in lukewarm water. Stir in eggs. Sift together remaining ingredients. Add to mixture. Refrigerate overnight. Divide dough. Place in two greased loaf pans. Drizzle with melted butter. Bake at 350° about 30 minutes. Cool. Slice thickly. Toast. Spread with butter and serve.

SPICEY PLUMS

Ingredients:

2 quarts plums
½ cup vinegar
2 cups sugar
1½ tsp. cinnamon
½ tsp. allspice
2 tsp. whole cloves

Directions:

Wash plums thoroughly. Cook with remaining ingredients until slightly soft. Chill in syrup and serve.

TIPSY PEACHES

Ingredients:

4 Tbl. butter
½ cup sugar
¼ cup water
4 fresh peaches, peeled
3 oz. brandy

Directions:

Melt butter and sugar in top of double boiler. Add water and peaches. Cook 30 minutes, stirring gently. Add brandy. Serve hot or cold.

MISS PRISSY'S SHERRIED FIG ICE CREAM

Ingredients:

4 eggs
¼ cup sugar
2 cups milk
3 Tbl. lemon juice
1 pint cream
½ cup sherry
1 tsp. vanilla
1 quart figs, crushed

Directions:

Beat eggs, milk, and sugar together. Cook in double boiler until slightly thickened. Stir constantly. Add remaining ingredients. Pour into five-quart ice cream freezer. Freeze until solid.

CONFEDERATE BUTTER BALLS

Ingredients:

1 cup butter, softened
2 cups flour
½ cup confectioners' sugar
¼ tsp. salt
1 cup pecan pieces
confectioners' sugar for garnish

Directions:

Mix ingredients. Shape into 1-inch balls. Place on greased cookie sheet. Bake at 350° until brown. Cool. Roll in confectioners' sugar.

50

PETITE PECAN TASSIES

Ingredients for 24 tassies:

Crust:
1 3-oz. package cream cheese, softened
½ cup butter, softened
1 cup flour, sifted
Filling:
1 egg, slightly beaten
¾ cup brown sugar
1 Tbl. butter, softened
1 tsp. vanilla
⅔ cup pecan pieces

Directions:

Mix crust ingredients. Chill at least 2 hours. Pinch off dough. Shape into 2 dozen 1-inch balls. Press balls into bottom and side of 1¾-inch muffin pans. Set aside.

Make filling: Mix all filling ingredients. Fill each crust 3/4 full. Bake at 325° for 25 minutes. Cool. Remove from pan.

LITTLE LADY LEMON PIES

Ingredients:

2 cups flour, sifted
1 tsp. salt
⅔ cup soft shortening (*not* butter, margarine, or vegetable oil)
4-6 Tbl. cold water
Filling:
2 cups sugar
2 Tbl. flour
6 eggs
2 Tbl. milk
3 Tbl. lemon juice
2 Tbl. butter, melted

Directions:

Sift flour and salt into bowl. Cut in ½ of shortening with 2 knives, until the mixture looks like coarse meal. Cut in remaining shortening, until it looks like large peas. Sprinkle water over mixture, 1 Tbl. at a time, and toss with fork until it clings together. Roll out dough on lightly floured board. Form flattened ball. With floured rolling pin, start in the center, and roll dough to the outside edge in all directions.

Cut into circles about 4 inches in diameter. These should slightly overlap the edge of the muffin tin, as you carefully place pastry inside it. Set aside.

Make filling: Mix flour and sugar. Beat in remaining ingredients. Pour filling into prepared, unbaked pastry shells. Bake at 350° until filling thickens and crust browns, about 30-45 minutes.

Holiday tables are bountiful and beautiful at Lovejoy

THANKSGIVING, CHRISTMAS, AND NEW YEAR'S AT LOVEJOY

Food plays a special part in the holiday festivities at Lovejoy. There is no better way to bring family and friends together than over a table that is covered with turkey, ham, and an array of sweets that'll have me signing up for the diet farm before New Year's.

We even decorate with food. This tradition really started with Louise Hastings (Mrs. Donald Hastings). Louise is a very talented floral designer and friend who has been decorating this house for parties and special occasions for years.

Her favorite Thanksgiving centerpiece is made with pineapples and grapes, because she says, "Fruit represents the abundance of Thanksgiving."

She uses a compote for the center of the table with oranges, apples, and lemons building up to a pineapple. Grapes spill out toward the ends of the table.

At Christmas, she designs a centerpiece around a Williamsburg apple tree. The apples are secured on a wooden cone-shaped form. Louise's apple tree is even prettier than the ones in Williamsburg, because she goes to great effort to find a variety of sizes of apples. She uses large ones around the base of the tree and graduates to smaller ones on each row going up. She crowns the tree with a small pineapple and fills in around the apples with boxwood.

Egg shells decorated like pigs make wonderful tree decorations

Making a gingerbread house is great holiday fun for the kids

As Louise says, "The fruit arrangements speak to the period of this house."

Sometimes the food I serve during the holidays provides an added decoration. I do a raw broccoli appetizer arranged in the shape of a wreath. I cut the top off of a red bell pepper and fill it with dip for the center of the wreath. The top of the pepper can be sliced into pieces and arranged as a bow at the bottom of the wreath. A parsley wreath filled with cherry tomatoes is another edible decoration Louise devised.

One of my favorite decorations gives us an excuse for a wonderful children's party. My friend Joyce Girod came up with this idea, and it has become a tradition for her two children and my grandchildren. We set up five or six card tables and provide the children with plenty of gingerbread and candies and they make Christmas houses for everyone.

Here are Joyce's instructions:

Cut out a pattern from thin cardboard according to the size and style house you want. Dust the cardboard with flour.

Blend one 14.5 ounce package of gingerbread mix with 1/3 cup lukewarm water. Chill one to two hours. Preheat oven to 375°. Roll dough 1/8 inch thick on floured, cloth-covered board. Keep unused dough refrigerated. Place cardboard pattern on dough and cut with sharp knife. Place on ungreased baking sheet. Bake at 375°, for twelve minutes for large pieces and five to seven minutes for small pieces.

Melt one cup granulated sugar in a shallow heavy skillet over low heat, stirring constantly. Keeping syrup over low heat, dip edge of house pieces in and quickly glue together. If glue hardens and won't stick, break off and start over.

For frosting, put two cups of confectioners' sugar in mixing bowl. Add 1 1/2 egg whites (about 3 tablespoons) that have been slightly beaten. Mix at lowest speed for one minute. Add 1 1/2 teaspoons white vinegar and beat at high speed for two minutes or until stiff and glossy. Spread frosting on house and let harden slightly. Press in candy.

Peppermint candy canes make an attractive rail fence, and pointed ice cream cones inverted and covered with green gumdrops make nice trees. Grated coconut can be used as snow.

Another fun food decoration is the pig tree. We blow extra-large eggs and decorate them to look like little pigs with angel wings. Pieces of pipe cleaners are coiled and stuck in one end to make a tail, and a button is glued on the other end for a nose. Construction paper is cut in the shapes of ears and wings. For legs, take about a quarter inch by two-inch strip of paper and roll tight and glue to the bottom of the egg shell. Glue a small yarn bow on top to hang them by.

These fun decorations make dining during the holidays all the more exciting.

Thanksgiving Talmadge Style

(for family and kissing cousins)

Celery Stalks
Stuffed Green Olives
Cranberry Salad
Brandy-Baked Thanksgiving Ham
Grandma Shingler's Scalloped Oysters
Turnip Greens with Fatback
City-Style Green Peas
Ocilla Candied Sweet Potatoes
Refrigerator Green Tomato Pickles
Criss-Cross Yeast Rolls
Pumpkin-Pecan Pie
Angel Food Cake with Ambrosia:
Fruits of the Gods
Charlotte Russe
Hot Coffee
Iced Tea

CRANBERRY SALAD

Ingredients:

1 lb. fresh cranberries
2 cups sugar
4 cups water
3 envelopes unflavored gelatin
1 lb. chutney
2 cups celery, chopped
2 cans (11 oz. each) mandarin
    oranges, drained

Directions:

Combine cranberries, sugar, and 2 cups water. Simmer 10 minutes. Mix gelatin with remaining 2 cups water. Stir gelatin mixture into hot cranberries. Chill until slightly thickened. Add chutney, celery, and oranges. Pour into a 2-quart mold. Chill until firm. To unmold, dip mold into lukewarm water for a second or two. Invert onto platter.

BRANDY-BAKED THANKSGIVING HAM

Ingredients:

1 Talmadge cured whole ham
1 quart apple juice
Glaze:
whole cloves
1 Tbl. prepared mustard
1 tsp. dry mustard
½ box brown sugar

juice of 2 oranges
½ cup brandy

Directions:

Place ham in covered roasting pan, fat side up. Add juice. Cover. Bake at 350° about 20 minutes per lb., or until done. Baste often.

Remove rind and some of fat. Score fat in diamond shapes. Stud with cloves. Spread on remaining glaze ingredients. Return to oven. Bake at 450° for 8-10 minutes, or until sugar melts and glazes surface.

GRANDMA SHINGLER'S SCALLOPED OYSTERS

Ingredients:

1½ pints fresh oysters
8 Tbl. butter, melted
2 cups Saltine cracker crumbs
about 1 cup half-and-half
½ tsp. salt
½ tsp. Worcestershire sauce
pepper

Directions:

Drain oysters. Save the liquor. Butter a shallow baking dish. Pour the melted butter over the crumbs. Toss lightly with a fork.

Spread 1/3 crumbs on bottom of baking dish. Cover with 1/2 the oysters. Sprinkle with pepper.

Layer another 1/3 of the crumbs and rest of oysters. Sprinkle with pepper.

Combine oyster liquor with enough half-and-half to make 1 cup liquid. Add salt and Worcestershire sauce. Pour over casserole. Top with remaining crumbs. Bake at 350° for 30 minutes.

TURNIP GREENS WITH FATBACK

Ingredients:

4 lbs. turnip greens
water for cooking
¼ lb. fatback
sugar
salt

Directions:

Boil fatback in large pot of water. Wash greens. Add greens. Simmer, covered, 2-3 hours. Add sugar and salt to taste. Serve with hot pepper sauce.

CITY-STYLE GREEN PEAS

Ingredients:

2 cans Le Seur brand tiny green English peas
salt
pepper
butter

Directions:

Open cans. Pour into sauce pan. Add remaining ingredients. Heat to boiling. Serve.

Talmadge Tip:

When we were children, we thought it was a real treat to have store-bought peas.

OCILLA CANDIED SWEET POTATOES

Ingredients
for 4 servings:

4 medium sweet potatoes, peeled
1 cup sugar
½ cup butter
water
½ tsp. salt

Directions:

Cut potatoes into 2-inch slices. Put in wide, heavy skillet. Add water ¼ of the way up. Cover. Cook slowly until tender. Drain water from pan. Sprinkle with sugar, butter, and salt. Cook slowly, uncovered, until liquid is sticky.

REFRIGERATOR GREEN TOMATO PICKLES

Ingredients:

3½ lbs. green tomatoes, sliced about ¼ inch thick
1 gallon water
½ cup lime
Syrup:
2 lbs. sugar
3 cups white vinegar
½ tsp. cloves
½ tsp. ginger
½ tsp. allspice
½ Tbl. celery seed
small cinnamon stick

Directions: Soak tomatoes in lime water 24 hours. Drain. Rinse. Soak 4 hours in clear water, rinsing and changing water every hour.

Bring syrup ingredients to a boil. Add tomatoes. Boil 1 hour. Chill and marinate overnight. Will keep several weeks in refrigerator.

Talmadge Tip: Use enamel or stainless steel pans, not aluminum, as it reacts with ingredients.

CRISS-CROSS YEAST ROLLS

Ingredients:

1 package dry yeast
1 cup warm water
1 cup warm milk
2 Tbl. shortening
2 Tbl. sugar
2 tsp. salt
5-6 cups flour
oil

Directions:

Dissolve yeast in water and milk. Add shortening, sugar, and salt. Beat in flour, 1 cup at a time, until dough is stiff. Brush with oil. Let rise in warm place until doubled in size. Turn out on floured board. Knead in as much flour as dough will absorb. Let rise 15 minutes. Punch down. Knead until smooth. Roll into 2-inch thickness. Cut with biscuit cutter. Place on greased cookie sheet. Slash tops in an "X" with sharp knife or scissors. Brush with water. Put in cold oven. Bake at 375° about 20 minutes, or until rolls are light brown.

PUMPKIN-PECAN PIE

Ingredients:

1 unbaked pie shell

Filling:
2 cups cooked pumpkin
⅔ cup dark brown sugar, packed
⅓ cup white sugar
2 tsp. cinnamon
1 tsp. ginger
½ tsp. nutmeg
¼ tsp. ground cloves
¼ tsp. mace
3 eggs
1 cup heavy cream
¼ cup milk
¼ cup bourbon whiskey

Topping:
¾ cup pecans, chopped
3 Tbl. butter, softened
2 Tbl. dark brown sugar

Directions:

Bake crust at 350° for 10 minutes. Do *not* brown.

Make filling: Mix ingredients with electric mixer. Pour filling into baked pie crust. Bake at 350° for 35 minutes.

Make topping: Mix ingredients. Spoon topping around edge. Bake again at 350° for 20-25 minutes, or until a knife inserted in center comes out clean. Chill.

AMBROSIA: FRUITS OF THE GODS

Ingredients:

2 dozen large oranges
6 bananas
2 8-oz. packages grated coconut
1 small jar red maraschino
   cherries
about ½ cup sugar

Directions:

Saving the juice; peel, section, and seed oranges. Put in punch bowl with juice. Peel and slice bananas. Add coconut and cherries. Sweeten to taste (oranges vary in sweetness). Refrigerate.

CHARLOTTE RUSSE

Ingredients
for 6 servings:

½ Tbl. gelatin
¼ cup cold milk
¼ cup warm milk
1 pint whipping cream
1 tsp. vanilla
½ cup sugar
sherry
5 egg whites, beaten stiff
ladyfingers, split

Directions:

Soften gelatin in cold milk. Dissolve in warm milk. Whip cream until stiff. Add vanilla, sugar, and sherry to taste. Add gelatin. Fold in egg whites. Pour into bowl or dessert glasses lined with ladyfingers.

Lovejoy Plantation Christmas

(for friendly drop-ins)

Company's Comin' Egg Nog
Nesselrode Pudding
Louise Hastings' Fruitcake
Christmas Coconut Cake
Miniature Ham Biscuits with
Sweet-Hot Mustard Sauce

COMPANY'S COMIN' EGG NOG

Ingredients
for 40 punch cups:

12 eggs, separated
1 cup sugar
1 cup bourbon whiskey
1 cup cognac
½ tsp. salt
3 pints heavy cream, whipped
nutmeg, grated

Directions:

With electric mixer, beat yolks and sugar. Slowly add bourbon and cognac. Chill. Beat egg whites and salt to form soft peaks. Fold egg whites and whipped cream into yolk mixture. Chill at least one hour. To serve, pour into punch bowl. Sprinkle with freshly grated nutmeg.

Talmadge Tip:

This egg nog is so thick, you'll want to eat it with a spoon.

NESSELRODE PUDDING

Ingredients:

2 envelopes plain gelatin
1 cup cold water
1 cup hot water
3 egg yolks
1 cup sugar
2 cups milk
½ cup raisins
3 Tbl. nuts, chopped
½ cup coconut, grated
1½ tsp. rum flavoring
3 egg whites, beaten stiff
whipped cream for garnish
holly leaves

Directions:

Soak gelatin in cold water. Dissolve in hot water. Beat yolks with sugar. Scald milk. Slowly add to yolks. Add remaining ingredients, folding in egg whites last. Pour into fancy mold. Chill. Garnish with whipped cream and holly leaves.

LOUISE HASTINGS' FRUITCAKE

Ingredients:

½ lb. red cherries
½ lb. green cherries
½ lb. red pineapple
½ lb. green pineapple
½ cup bourbon whiskey

1 lb. chopped nuts
½ cup flour
¾ lb. butter
2 cups sugar
6 eggs
3½ cups flour
2 tsp. baking powder
¼ tsp. salt
2 Tbl. vanilla

Directions:

The night before, cut up fruit. Marinate in bourbon. Mix nuts with ½ cup flour. Let stand overnight. Next morning, cream butter and sugar. Beat in eggs. Sift dry ingredients together. Stir in. Fold in marinated fruit and nuts. Pour into greased loaf pans lined with heavy brown paper. Bake at 250° for 1½-2 hours.

CHRISTMAS COCONUT CAKE

Ingredients:

1 cup butter
2 cups sugar
3½ cups cake flour, sifted
2 heaping tsp. baking powder
1 cup buttermilk
7 egg whites, fluffed up
1 tsp. vanilla
1 tsp. lemon juice
Filling:
2 cups sugar
1 cup cold water
2 Tbl. white Karo syrup
3 egg whites, stiffly beaten
2 tsp. sugar
2 coconuts, grated

Directions:

Cream butter. Add sugar. Cream *thoroughly.* Sift flour and baking powder. Add alternately with milk. Fold in egg whites. Pour into 2 8-inch, square pans, heavily greased and floured. Bake at 375° for 30-35 minutes. Cool in pans for 10 minutes. Remove to wire racks.

Make filling: Cook sugar, water and Karo syrup until it spins long thread. Beat egg whites with 2 tsp. sugar. Fold syrup mixture into beaten egg whites. Add most of coconut. Fill and cover cake. Sprinkle remaining coconut on top.

MINIATURE HAM BISCUITS

Ingredients: Rhett Butler's Biscuits (page 13), already prepared (the dough should be cut with a 2-inch biscuit cutter)
Talmadge Country Ham, baked and shaved wafer-thin
Sweet-Hot Mustard Sauce

Directions: Split open biscuits. Generously spread with sauce. Cover with ham and top half of biscuits.

SWEET-HOT MUSTARD SAUCE

Ingredients: 1 cup Coleman's mustard
1 cup apple cider vinegar
1 cup sugar
3 eggs

Directions: Soak mustard and vinegar overnight. Add sugar and eggs. Cook in double boiler until thick.

New Year's Day Supper

(for folks who want greenbacks, good luck,
and pennies in the new year)

Hot Pot Likker
Ringin'-in-the-New-Year Relishes
Barbecued Spareribs
Blazin' Barbecue Sauce
Black-Eyed Peas with Hog Jowl
Rutabaga Turnips   Greenback Collards
Tomato Marmalade
Green and Red Pepper Jelly
Bentley's Homemade Bran Bread
'Cile's Corn Pones
Southern Gingerbread with Caramel Sauce
Coffee
Hot Tea

HOT POT LIKKER

Ingredients
for 5-6 servings: 1 quart liquid from cooked collards
1 Tbl. lemon juice
heavy dash Tabasco sauce
salt
pepper
thin lemon slices for garnish

Directions: Skim fat from liquid. Add seasonings. Bring to a boil. To serve,
ladle into small cups. Float lemon
on top.

RINGIN'-IN-THE-NEW-YEAR RELISHES

Ingredients: cucumbers
yellow squash
green peppers
onions
carrots
radishes
prepared champagne- or wine-
flavored salad dressing

Directions: Cut all fresh vegetables in
rings. Chill in ice water. Pour
dressing into "dip" cup. Sur-
round with raw vegetables.

BARBECUED SPARERIBS

Ingredients:
4 lbs. ribs, cut into pieces of 5-6 ribs each
water to cook
2 tsp. salt
1 Tbl. vinegar
Blazin' Barbecue Sauce

Directions:
Place ribs in heavy Dutch oven. Cover with water. Add salt and vinegar. Bring to a boil. Cover. Simmer 20 minutes. Drain. Spread ribs on broiler pan. Baste with Blazin' Barbecue Sauce. Broil 6-8 inches from heat for 15 minutes, turning and basting every 5 minutes. Watch carefully to prevent burning.

BLAZIN' BARBECUE SAUCE

See recipe on page 28.

BLACK-EYED PEAS WITH HOG JOWL

Ingredients:

1 lb. black-eyed peas
water to cover
½ lb. hog jowl
2 quarts water
salt
pepper

Directions:

Cover peas with water. Bring to boil. Turn off heat. Let sit 1½ hours or overnight. Drain. Boil hog jowl in 2 quarts water for 1 hour. This extracts juice and reduces liquid. Skim fat. Add drained peas. Simmer about ½ hour, until tender, but not mushy. Season with salt and pepper.

GREENBACK COLLARDS

Ingredients
for 6 servings:

1½ lbs. collard greens
2 quarts water
¾ lb. ham hock
½ tsp. salt
1 tsp. sugar
¼ tsp. cayenne pepper

Directions:

Wash collards thoroughly. Remove stalks. Cover with water. Add ham and seasonings. Cook over medium heat until tender, about 1 hour. Drain, reserving liquid for Hot Pot Likker. Chop with scissors.

Talmadge Tip:

Collards are much better after being nipped by frost. If Jack Frost hasn't touched your garden, place in freezer 20-30 minutes before cooking.

RUTABAGA TURNIPS

Ingredients for
about 25 servings:

1 slice country-cured ham hock
4 cups water
1 large or 2 medium rutabagas (yellow)

4-5 turnips (white)
salt
pepper
pinch of sugar
3 Tbl. lemon juice
3-4 Tbl. butter

Directions:

Boil ham hock in water 30-40 minutes. Peel and slice rutabagas and turnips. Simmer all ingredients except butter 1-1½ hours. Remove ham hock. Mash rutabagas and turnips with potato masher. Add butter. Mash again. Serve with ham hock.

Talmadge Tip:

We usually cook this a day or so ahead, refrigerate, and reheat to serve. Great with Tomato Marmalade.

TOMATO MARMALADE

Ingredients:

2 cups canned tomatoes, undrained
1 large can tomato sauce
¼ cup butter
1 cup brown sugar
1 cup honey
juice of 2 to 3 lemons
juice of 1 orange
salt
pepper

Directions:

Bring all ingredients to a boil in
a large skillet. Reduce heat. Stir
and simmer about 1 hour, or until
sauce is thick.

GREEN AND RED PEPPER JELLY

Ingredients:

½ cup hot red peppers, seeded
and coarsely chopped
½ cup hot green peppers, seeded
and coarsely chopped
1 medium onion, quartered
1½ cups vinegar
5½ cups sugar
1 bottle liquid pectin

Directions:

Finely process peppers, onion,
and vinegar in food processor.
Put mixture and sugar in 6-quart

pot. Boil 1 minute. Remove from heat. Add pectin. Stir and skim foam for 5 minutes. Ladle into hot, sterilized jars. Shake to keep peppers mixed. Cool.

Talmadge Tip:

Many Southerners keep pepper sauce on their tables and put a dash of it on everything they eat. Pepper jelly is piquant but more refined, and is often seen, green- or red-colored, on top of cream cheese spread on crackers. It is also excellent with country ham.

BENTLEY'S HOMEMADE BRAN BREAD

Ingredients:

1 cup 100 percent bran cereal
1 cup cold water
½ cup hot water (100°-105°)
1 Tbl. honey
3 packages granulated yeast
1 Tbl. salt
1 cup hot water
1¾ cups dry milk powder
1 small package sunflower seeds
2 Tbl. poppy seeds
½ cup oil
⅔ cup honey
2 eggs, beaten
6 cups mixed bread flour (3 cups unbleached white flour, 2½ cups whole wheat flour, and ½ cup rye flour)

Directions:

In large mixing bowl, soak bran in cold water. In small bowl, mix ½ cup hot water with 1 Tbl. honey. Add yeast. Allow to foam. Mix all ingredients with soaked bran, adding flour 1 cup at a time. Knead until smooth and elastic, adding more flour, if needed. Place in greased bowl. Cover. Allow to rise until tripled in bulk. Punch down. Shape into four loaves. Place in greased loaf pans. Allow to rise until doubled in bulk. Bake at 350° for 25-30 minutes.

'CILE'S CORN PONES

Ingredients:

2 cups cornmeal
1 tsp. sugar
1 Tbl. shortening
warm water

Directions:

Sift dry ingredients. Cut in shortening. Add enough warm water to make a soft dough. Pinch off biscuit-sized pieces. Shape and flatten with your hands to about ½ inch thick. Place corn pones in greased iron skillet. Broil until tops brown. Reduce heat to 375°. Bake about 15 minutes.

SOUTHERN GINGERBREAD WITH CARAMEL SAUCE

Ingredients:

½ cup sugar
½ cup butter and lard, mixed
1 egg
1 cup dark syrup
1 tsp. cinnamon
½ tsp. salt
1 tsp. ginger
½ tsp. cloves
2½ cups flour
1½ tsp. soda
1 cup hot water

Caramel Sauce:
3 Tbl. butter
3 Tbl. flour
1½ cups sugar
2 cups water

Directions:

Cream sugar into butter. Add egg and syrup. Sift remaining dry ingredients. Add alternately with water. Pour into greased 9-inch, square pan. Bake at 350° for 25-30 minutes. (Test for doneness with toothpick.)

Make Caramel Sauce: Cream butter and flour. Caramelize sugar by melting over low heat, stirring until browned. Add water slowly. Cook until bubbly. Add to butter and flour. Pour over Southern Gingerbread, to serve.

Painting a treehouse (and each other) can work up an appetite

KIDS, ANIMALS, GOOD TIMES, AND GOOD FOOD

Sitting out here under these old oaks, it's hard to believe there is a huge, bustling city down the road. The quails are talking to each other, and there is a breeze whispering through the magnolia leaves. This old house seems to be resting for a moment.

But any minute now, my grandchildren will arrive and I'll feel like I'm right smack in the middle of a Mardi Gras parade. I am about to give my favorite party, a party that has become an annual tradition in this family.

Some years ago, when my grandchildren — Herman III, Tyler, Mit, Robert, and Libby — were quite young, I hired a carpenter to build a treehouse for them. We had an understanding that the children would be involved in the work.

Little Herman, the oldest of my grandchildren, was more than willing to help. He said, "Grandma, you hold the nail and I'll hit it."

I said, "Oh, no, Herman. You hold the nail and *I'll* hit it!"

It took a long time to get the treehouse built, because the carpenter spent more time watching the children than he did on his job.

When they finally finished, I decided the children should paint it. They invited a dozen of their friends over, and I warned the mothers to dress them in the

Billy T. Sherman is often an uninvited guest at parties

Rabbit E. Lee's home is a miniature Southern mansion

oldest clothes they owned. Armed with three gallons of water-soluble green paint and plenty of brushes, they went to work on the treehouse. Predictably enough, they ended up painting each other.

During all of this, their grandfather was in the house participating in an awards ceremony that included visiting dignitaries and members of the press. It didn't take long for the photographers to abandon the dignitaries and come outside to take pictures of the children. Those photographs are among my most prized possessions.

It took me four hours to get those children clean enough to put in a car. But we all had so much fun that day, the children insisted we had to do it again the next year. The painting party has remained pretty much the same each year. Except for last year when they decided to paint me.

Fortunately, my grandchildren are close by. One reason they love coming here is to play with my wild collection of animals, known around here as "the plantation personnel."

About all the work they do is greet the guests. When Erma Bombeck came here to visit, she arrived to a welcoming committee that consisted of Rabbit E. Lee, Ulysses S. Grunt, Billy T. Sherman, Clark Gobble, Scarlett O'Hen, Ruff Butler, and a peacock who answers to the name Uncle Pretty Pat.

I had planned a dinner party that evening honoring Erma and Liz Carpenter and a beautiful Saudi Arabian princess who lives in Atlanta. As Erma, Liz, and I walked out onto the terrace, a helicopter landed on the lawn, and out stepped Princess Asiya Saud Al Kabir. Erma turned to me and said, "This is the ultimate extreme —

from a goat and a pig on one side of the house to a princess and a helicopter on the other!"

We all had a good laugh, and I guess that's what the plantation personnel are best at. They do make people smile. When I have a barbecue, I tie a bow around Ulysses S. Grunt's neck and the children argue over who gets to walk him around. They have a ball and so does everyone else.

Ulysses has acquired fairly nice party manners, but I'm afraid we can't say the same for Billy T. Sherman. Billy is a likeable old goat who sleeps on the front porch under my window and eats my geraniums. He also eats tablecloths and napkins. He recently broke loose during one of my parties, and when a friend tried to bribe him with a paper plate of chicken scraps, he ate the plate and turned up his nose at the chicken. I think he's trying to ruin my reputation for fried chicken.

What Billy wants most is to be where the action is. My cat, Jonas Wilkerson — known around here as the manager of the plantation — is the same way. They say pets take on their owners' personalities, and I guess mine prove it.

Last year during the Midtown Connection celebration, an annual event held in Atlanta by the Georgia Trust for Historic Preservation, they really got to be the center of attention. The children and some friends loaded all of them into trucks and took them downtown to the party. Clark Gobble and Scarlett O'Hen, a charming couple from a prominent Southern family of turkeys, went along, and Scarlett got so excited she laid an egg on Peachtree Street. Atlanta historian Franklin Garrett said it has to be the first egg laid on Peachtree since 1837 (the year Atlanta was incorporated). And I

Princess Asiya Saud Al Kabir arrived by helicopter

guess maybe it'll be the last.

Scarlett O'Hen certainly won't be laying another one there. It took me two days and several trucks to get all of them and their houses and fences to town.

Naming the animals has gotten to be a game for many of the people who have visited Lovejoy.

After Erma was here, she sent me a hot water bottle shaped like a lamb with a note that said, "I'm not smart enough to come up with a name like Billy T. Sherman, but would you please accept Abaaaham Lincoln from a grateful Yankee?"

Since then, we have gotten Edgar Allan Crow, who also doesn't sound Southern, but at least he likes my fried chicken.

Kids' Things

(for little kids and old goats)

Pigs on a Stick with
Horseback Sauce
Hen Legs in Bean Beds
Ruff's Painted Hush Puppies
Back Yard Corn on the Cob
Rainbow Sugar Cookies
Billy T. Sherman's Chocolate Glutton Pie
Watermelon Slices
Ice Cream Cones
Gorp by Sam B.
Pink Lemonade
Strawberry Smoothies

PIGS ON A STICK

Ingredients:

1 cup pancake mix
2 Tbl. cornmeal
1 Tbl. sugar
1 tsp. salt
⅔ cup water
1 lb. pork hot dogs
fat for deep frying
sticks (one for each "pig")

Directions:

Mix dry ingredients and water. Dip hot dogs into mixture. Fry in hot fat until brown. Drain. Insert sticks. Serve with Horseback Sauce.

Talmadge Tip:

Better still, I say, save time and buy Talmadge Farms Corndogs.

HORSEBACK SAUCE

Ingredients:

1 Tbl. prepared horseradish
1 Tbl. prepared mustard
4 cups catsup
1 tsp. lemon juice
1 tsp. Worcestershire sauce
salt

Directions:

Mix ingredients. Serve with Pigs on a Stick.

Talmadge Tip:

Reduce horseradish if sauce is strictly for the children.

HEN LEGS IN BEAN BEDS

*Ingredients
for 8 servings:*

6 cups canned pork and beans
heavy aluminum foil
8-16 drumsticks and drumettes
salt
¼ cup unsulphured molasses
2 Tbl. prepared mustard
¼ cup corn oil
¼ cup vinegar
2 Tbl. Worcestershire sauce
¼ cup catsup

Directions:

Put about ⅔ cup of beans on large sheet of foil. Lay on 1 drumstick or 2 drumettes. Generously brush chicken and beans with sauce made of remaining ingredients. Close pouches tightly. Place on cookie sheet. Bake at 350° about 25 minutes.

RUFF'S PAINTED HUSH PUPPIES

Ingredients:

2 cups cornbread mix
   (plus egg, water, etc., according to package directions)
¾ cup finely minced raw vegetables
   (green pepper, onion, cabbage, broccoli, squash, etc.)
bacon grease for frying
chili sauce or catsup

Directions:

Make up cornbread according to package directions. Add minced vegetables. Drop by small spoonfuls into hot fat. When brown, turn and brown other side. Brush these little, flat hush puppies with chili sauce or catsup to serve.

Talmadge Tip:

This is a great way to get children to try new vegetables. The chili sauce adds Vitamin A and contains less sugar than catsup.

BACK YARD CORN ON THE COB

Ingredients: corn on the cob, still in the shucks
                        water for cooking
                        salt
                        butter

Directions: Drop unshucked ears into boil-
                        ing water. Boil 5-7 minutes, ac-
                        cording to size of ears. Drain. Let
                        children shuck, salt, and butter
                        their own ears — outdoors.

Talmadge Tip: The silks pull back with the
                        shucks. The shuck makes a "han-
                        dle." No corn holders need to be
                        used.

RAINBOW SUGAR COOKIES

Ingredients: 2 cups butter
                        1 cup sugar
                        1 cup brown sugar
                        2 eggs
                        1 tsp. almond flavoring
                        4 cups flour
                        1 tsp. soda
                        ½ tsp. salt
                        few drops of yellow, green, blue,
                            and red food colorings

Directions: Cream butter and sugars. Add

98

eggs and flavoring. Sift dry ingredients together. Add gradually. Divide into 4 equal batches. Tint each batch a different color by kneading in food coloring (children can do this themselves). Shape into 1-inch balls. Place on cookie sheet. Bake at 375° for 10-12 minutes.

BILLY T. SHERMAN'S CHOCOLATE GLUTTON PIE

Ingredients for 6 servings:

1 square unsweetened baker's chocolate
¼ cup butter
1 cup sugar
2 eggs, slightly beaten
1 Tbl. vanilla
1 unbaked pie shell

Directions:

Melt chocolate with butter (do not let boil). Stir in sugar. Cool slightly. Add eggs and vanilla. Pour into unbaked pie shell. Bake at 300° for 35 minutes.

GORP BY SAM B.

Ingredients: 1 8-oz. package of M&M choco-
                     late candies
                  1 8-oz. jar roasted peanuts
                  ½ cup raisins

Directions: Mix and eat.

Talmadge Tip: Jimmy Bentley says of this mix
                  his son invented, "It gives kids
                  instant energy . . . as if they
                  needed it!"

STRAWBERRY SMOOTHIES

Ingredients: ½ cup strawberries, sliced
                  2 cups milk
                  2 tsp. sugar
                  ¼ tsp. vanilla flavoring
                  3-4 ice cubes

Directions: Put all ingredients in blender.
                  Blend and serve.

Talmadge Tip: Add an egg and/or yogurt for
                  extra nourishment. Other fruits
                  such as ripe bananas, peaches, or
                  pineapple can be used separately
                  or in combination.

TROTTERS, TALES, AND OTHER WILD WEEDS

I come from a long line of good Southern cooks. My Mama made the best chicken pie I've ever eaten, and my Aunt Lillie Shingler earned her living serving good food. She owned a guest house in Ashburn, Georgia, called "The House By the Road". Even Duncan Hines was very impressed by her food. He visited there on several occasions and included some of Aunt Lillie's recipes in his cookbooks.

But somehow I grew up knowing what good food was, but having no earthly idea how to cook it. Mama didn't like to have anybody around when she was in the kitchen. And when we visited Aunt Lillie, there was too much going on for me to be interested in how she made waffles.

And so, the first meal I cooked as an eighteen-year-old newlywed Navy bride was not a menu that ought to be in this cookbook. It consisted of a broiled steak, canned peas, boiled carrots and a store-bought strawberry shortcake. I spent an entire day fixing that meal, and it was awful.

I didn't know what was wrong; all I knew was that it didn't taste like anything I had grown up eating. Unfortunately, I couldn't run next door to ask Mama or Aunt Lillie what went wrong, because I was living in New York at the time.

I eventually learned how to cook Mama's chicken pie and Aunt Lillie's waffles and some other things I

Jimmy Bentley serves up a helping of his Brunswick stew

never thought I'd want to cook. Things like quail, chitlins, souse meat, and even possum — things that come with the territory.

When I moved to Lovejoy, I became interested in the plantation foods that are so much a part of the Southern heritage. On the plantation, anything that was edible eventually made its way to the table, be it game from the hunt or poke sallet from the yard. When a hog was killed, nothing was thrown out; every piece of meat and fat got used in something.

Bird hunting was a great sport for the plantation men, but it also meant a special supper of quail.

For years I couldn't understand why people considered quail such a delicacy. My former husband went bird hunting a lot, and every time he brought quail home, I'd throw them in the freezer and try to forget about them. One day, my friend Gretchen Byrd said, "Betty, if you're not ever going to cook those birds, I'd love to have them." I gave them to her and she invited us over to try them. They were out of this world. The secret, she said, was to soak them in salt water and then use wine and lemon juice during the cooking. I'm sorry I didn't know that sooner. I think maybe I hadn't liked the dry taste, and her recipe took that away.

It's funny how squeamish we can be about the foods our forefathers and mothers survived on. If you just mention pickled pigs feet or explain what chitlins are to some people, their appetites are ruined for the day.

When my old friend Jimmy Bentley's daughter Betty, my namesake, was a debutante, I decided to have a party for her. I served barbecued pork, but for fun I put a big ceramic mama possum with baby possums on her back in the middle of the tray. I told the girls we were

Was it possum or barbecue? The debutantes weren't sure

having good old barbecued possum. Bless those little debutantes' hearts! They kept looking at that meat and looking back at me, and finally one said, "Mrs. Talmadge, is that *really* possum?"

I'm not crazy about possum, either, but I've eaten it. And frankly, I knew the first time I smelled chitlins cooking I didn't like them. But I'm a history buff in a sense. And I hope the recipes for all those old country foods will continue to be handed down for a lot more generations to come.

Trotters, Tales, and Wild Weeds

(old-timey recipes for the new times)

Trotters, Pickled
Sawmill Chicken
Country Cracklins
Chitlins
Grandma Shingler's Liver Puddin'
Head Cheese Loaf
Liver Sausage
Mild Country Farm Sausage
Hot Country Farm Sausage
Jimmy's Brunswick Stew
Poke Salad Sambo
Poke Salit Helen
Hoecakes
Ferrol's Vegetable Garden Soup
Pomegranate Jelly
Old-Fashioned Quincedonia Preserves
Roast 'Possum

TROTTERS, PICKLED (alias Pickled Pigs' Feet)

Ingredients:

pigs' feet
clean brick
Brine:
1 lb. salt
¼ lb. sugar
¼ oz. saltpeter
9 cups water

Directions:

Thoroughly wash freshly cleaned, chilled pigs' feet (alias "trotters"). Make up the brine. Put in the feet. Weight them with the clean brick to keep them down in the solution. Let cure for 15 days-3 weeks at 36°-40°.

Cook and serve (see recipe for Agony of deFeet).

SAWMILL CHICKEN (alias Fried Salt Pork)

*Ingredients for 2-3
servings:*

2 tsp. lard or shortening
¾ lb. fatback, thinly sliced
½ cup buttermilk
½-¾ cup flour
½ tsp. pepper

Directions:

Heat the lard in an iron skillet. Dip each slice of fatback into buttermilk. Dust in flour and pepper. Fry until golden brown. Turn once. Do not crowd pieces. Drain on paper towel.

COUNTRY CRACKLINS

Ingredients:	1 lb. fatback or fat off fresh ham ½ cup water
Directions:	Since few stores have fresh cracklins, here's how to render them fit to add to cornbread. Cut fatback into small pieces. Put in a pot with water. Cook and stir until water is gone and the small pieces of fat are crisp and brown. (Do not confuse these with chitlins.) Add to cornbread for extra flavor and texture.
Talmadge Tip:	The leftover liquid fat will congeal, when chilled. This is "lard." It can be used for shortening or fat in cooking.

CHITLINS

Ingredients:	5 lbs. chitlins onion water salt pepper
Directions:	Clean chitlins well. Place with an onion in a deep pot. Add just enough water to cover (salted and peppered to taste). Simmer gently until tender, about 2 or 3 hours. Drain and serve. Some people like to eat these plain; some like to batter and fry them.
Talmadge Tip:	I once heard that Craig Claiborne, the *New York Times* food expert, said that he would like to find a good way to cook chitlins. I agree. I'm not a great chitlins lover myself, but I do serve them, if I'm forced to. Just knowing that chitlins are the small intestines of a hog puts off some people when it comes to preparing or eating them. It is best to cook chitlins a day ahead, unless you have a good neighbor with a well-ventilated kitchen and no sense of smell! I was once told that the smell can

be reduced by boiling 2-3 whole, unshelled pecans in the water as the chitlins are cooked.

Good luck, and don't call me!

GRANDMA SHINGLER'S LIVER PUDDIN'

Ingredients:

1 hog liver
hog lights (lung)
1 hog jowl
1½-2 cups cooked rice
1 medium onion, finely chopped
salt
pepper

Directions:

Simmer together liver, lights, and jowl until tender. Remove meat from jowl. Cut by hand into small pieces. Grind in food chopper. Add rice and onion. Salt and pepper to taste. Mix well. Pack into a bowl or loaf pan. Refrigerate.

Talmadge Tip:

There's no product on the market today that compares with this old-fashioned standby.

HEAD CHEESE LOAF

Ingredients:

pigs' heads
pigs' tongues
pigs' hearts
other organ pieces
water
salt
black pepper
red pepper
ground cloves
coriander
sweet marjoram

Directions:

Use pigs' heads, tongues, hearts, and other organ pieces. Make deep cuts in thick pieces. Cover with water and simmer until the meat slips easily from the bones and practically falls to pieces. Remove bones. Grind. Return to the broth. Bring to a boil. This reheating mixes the head cheese and makes it thicker. Add seasoning. Simmer 30 minutes. Pour into loaf pans. Chill. Store in refrigerator. Head cheese is usually eaten cold. It is sliced and often served with vinegar.

Talmadge Tip:

Old timers attribute good health and long life to all the vitamins and minerals in this dish.

110

LIVER SAUSAGE

Ingredients:

pigs' head
pigs' hearts
pigs' tongues
pigs' livers
water
salt
pepper
herbs and spices to taste

Directions:

Make deep cuts in thick pieces. Simmer heads, tongues, hearts, and other pieces in water to cover. Remove from heat as soon as meat can be boned. Bone meat. (Scald livers about 10 minutes.) Grind all cooked meat moderately finely. Add enough liquid from cooked meat to make mixture soft, but not sloppy. Season with salt, pepper, herbs, and spices. Mix thoroughly. Simmer 30 minutes. Put in loaf pan or mold. Chill.

MILD COUNTRY FARM SAUSAGE

Ingredients:

50 lbs. pork, chopped into 1-inch cubes
11 oz. salt
1½ oz. black pepper, medium grind
1½ oz. rubbed sage
½ oz. ground red pepper
½ oz. crushed red pepper
1 oz. light brown sugar

Directions:

Mix meat with seasonings. Put through a grinder, using as sharp a blade as possible, so that the fat is not crushed. While working, keep it *cold* (temperature should be as close to 34° as possible). Freeze in rolls, patties, or loaves of suitable size for your family.

Talmadge Tip:

Don't try to make lean sausage. It *must* be at least 40 percent fat.

HOT COUNTRY FARM SAUSAGE

Use the same ingredients and instructions as for Mild Country Farm Sausage, adding 1 oz. more of ground red pepper.

Talmadge Tip:

Sausage is really not all that

hard to make. Today's food pro-
cessors take all of the work out of
the grinding.

JIMMY'S BRUNSWICK STEW

Ingredients:

1 gallon cooked chicken, chopped
½ gallon cooked pork, chopped
1½ gallons tomatoes (fresh or
 canned), peeled
2 gallons corn, mixture of cream
 style and whole kernel
1 large bottle catsup
1 gallon chicken broth
6-8 onions, chopped and sautéed
1 cup brown sugar
3 jiggers salt
2-3 jiggers black pepper
2 cups Blazin' Barbecue Sauce

Directions:

Place all ingredients in big,
black iron washpot. Simmer
slowly about half the day (6-10
hours) until it's thick enough to
eat with a fork. Taste. If it needs
more seasoning, add a little pepper, salt, or Blazin' Barbecue
Sauce.

113

POKE SALAD SAMBO

Poke is a wild weed that grows in country fields and city ivy beds. When prepared properly, it is quite a delectable green — much like fresh spinach. Legend has it that Southern plantation owners learned to eat poke salad after the War Between the States, when the horrors of Reconstruction forced them into near-starvation.

The first requirement for poke salad is knowing how and when to gather it. It begins appearing in early April. Gather it while the stalks are not fully leafed out. This way it is not necessary to carry a knife into the yard or woods to cut it. It is so tender, it can be broken off. Break it off as far down as possible. One winds up with a pale pink stalk that resembles pink asparagus.

Wash a good mess of what you've collected. Pull off the leaves and drop in boiling, salted water. Parboil about 10 minutes. Drain, then boil 5 minutes more in water seasoned with salt pork or bacon strips.

This twice-cooked poke is served with Hoecake and some type of pork dish, like pork roast. Fried chicken is also good.

Talmadge Tip:
Dr. Ferrol Sams says this is just the way he cooks his home-grown poke weeds.

114

POKE SALIT HELEN

This is Dr. Helen Sams' way of spelling and preparing poke salad. Take the tall and tender stalks. Peel off the pink or red outer covering. Chop as you would okra. Roll the chopped pieces of poke salit stalks in seasoned cornmeal. Deep fry it as you would fry okra. This has quite a different flavor from the boiled poke salad—a little like asparagus.

The reason for parboiling the leaves and peeling the stems is the notion that poke is poisonous, if not prepared this way. I am not at all sure this is true, but I have never seen anyone come to any harm when they eat it after it has been cooked in these two fashions.

Also, to prevent frequent trotting to the outhouse, never gather poke if the stems have turned dark red, berries have formed, or the leaves are tough. A good way to tell if poke is too tough is to see if the stalk will snap between your fingers. If it just bends and does not snap, the weed is too old.

While this delicate, delicious dish may have originated in poverty, it has persisted as an epicurean item of snobbery in the South. Poke will drive yankees stark-raving crazy, but people with any Southern blood in them will relish it. Look out in your yard. You may find some poke thriving amongst the ivy and azaleas.

HOECAKES

Ingredients for 1 dozen:

1 cup white cornmeal
½ tsp. salt
¾ cup boiling water
2 Tbl. bacon drippings

Directions:

Combine cornmeal and salt. Slowly add water, stirring constantly. Beat until smooth. Heat bacon drippings in heavy griddle. When fat is very hot, drop batter into flat, round cakes. Fry a few minutes on each side until brown. Reduce heat, if necessary to prevent burning.

Talmadge Tip:

When all the eggs were used for breakfast or baking, this eggless cornbread was fixed for supper.

116

FERROL'S VEGETABLE GARDEN SOUP

Take a bottle of chicken bouillon. Dissolve it in about 6 quarts of boiling water. Use a great big cast iron or cast aluminum pot. Chop up two or three good-sized onions and at least one big bunch of celery. Put them into the boiling chicken broth. Blanch and peel a whole lot of very fresh tomatoes. Core and chop them into the pot. Then add some fresh okra, chopped. Let all of this boil real good until it begins to settle down.

Now cut corn off of 1 or 2 dozen ears. Boil this a while, until you think the corn is done. Add more water, if needed.

The very last thing to put in the soup is butterbeans. It is important that these are fresh. If they are tiny and a little underdeveloped, they are much more delicious. The trick is to boil the butterbeans separately. Then add them to the soup after it is done, after it has been removed from the heat to cool.

Taste along as you add the vegetables to be sure the seasonings are right. Put in extra water whenever needed. Do not get it too salty.

Ladle the soup into freezer cartons. Set aside and let cool. Refrigerate for 24 hours and then freeze. It keeps indefinitely. The soup's taste of fresh vegetables is much richer than just freezing the individual vegetables by themselves.

POMEGRANATE JELLY

The main trick here is preparing the fruit for cooking. Wear a pair of rubber gloves to shell pomegranates and extract their beautiful, ruby-red seeds. Otherwise, your fingertips and nails become hopelessly stained for days!

Get as many pomegranate seeds as you can manage. Run them through a food processor to extract the juice. Strain the juice to get the seeds out. Add a little cayenne pepper to the juice. Do this to taste, just barely enough cayenne to say, "My that's hot," not "Good God A'mighty, that's burning me up!"

Measure and mix the juice and sugar according to the directions on the Certo package. The secret to making this jelly jell is to boil it for 5 minutes instead of the "1 minute rolling boil" it says on the package.

This results in a beautiful, red jelly that is absolutely delicious dolloped on cream cheese or crackers. A few of these hors d'oeuvres with a cocktail will make any reasoning person understand why the Greek goddess Persephone was imprisoned in the underworld for a mere taste of pomegranate.

OLD-FASHIONED QUINCEDONIA PRESERVES

Take your quincedonias, wash them, break them in two with a hatchet. Slice them into strips, remove the peeling with a knife. Core them. Grate small pieces in hand-cranked food mill, like coconut. Add equal amount of sugar. Put on the stove and bring to a rolling boil for about 10 minutes. Taste to be sure your quincedonia pulp is tender.

Pour into sterilized fruit jars or jelly glasses. Seal as you would for any ordinary preserves or jelly. The result is a very tart, spicy jelly that is good either on English muffins for breakfast or as a side dish with meats. Prepared this way, the finished product is a beautiful yellowish-orange color that is as pretty as it is tasty.

Talmadge Tip:
This is Dr. Ferrol Sams' family's favorite breakfast.

ROAST 'POSSUM

Ingredients:

1 opossum, dressed
salt
pepper
1 onion, chopped
opossum liver, chopped
1 Tbl. fat
1 cup bread crumbs
1 hard-cooked egg, chopped
¼ tsp. Worcestershire sauce
1 tsp. salt
water to moisten stuffing
bacon slices
water to cook

Directions:

Rub opossum with salt and pepper. Sauté onion and chopped liver in fat. Mix in crumbs, egg, and seasonings. Add enough water to moisten. Stuff in opossum's cavity. Truss like a fowl. Put in uncovered roasting pan. Cover with bacon slices. Pour water into pan 1 inch deep. Bake at 350° until tender, about 2½ hours. Serve with baked sweet potatoes.

Talmadge Tip:

Opossum should be cleaned as soon as possible after shooting. It should be hung in a cool place for 48 hours. It is then ready to be skinned and cooked. The meat is light-colored and tender. Excess fat may be removed, but there is no strong flavor or odor contained in the fat.

ME AND MARILYN MONROE—MY MOVIE CAREER

A lot of crazy things have happened in my kitchen, and I've certainly had a few surprises there, but nothing will ever equal my "discovery." By Hollywood, that is.

I got discovered in my own kitchen. Me and Marilyn Monroe. And the next thing I knew, I was watching myself on television with Andy Griffith and Johnny Cash.

My day started off hectic because I was getting ready for a Magnolia Supper honoring Michio Watanabe, the Minister of Finance from Tokyo, Japan. I had gotten a call from somebody connected with the movie version of *Murder in Coweta County*, asking if they could come look for places to shoot some of the scenes. I thought that sounded exciting, and told them to come on out.

The handsome young director, Gary Nelson, arrived and we met, but I didn't pay much attention to what was going on, because I was busy finishing my arrangements for Mr. Watanabe's entourage.

The next day, Mr. Nelson's assistant called and said "Mrs. Talmadge, the director would like to have you in the movie." I thought I was hearing things. I let that sink in for a minute and said, "Honey, I've never even been in a high school play, much less a movie."

She asked me to come down to Griffin to the

A star is born: Andy Griffith (L), director Gary Nelson, and me

Holiday Inn to read some lines. I felt like Betty Talmadge, ingénue.

I arrived in Griffin and they presented me with a script. I read the lines and they signed me up. They told me I would be paid union scale even though I wasn't a member of the union. I was so delighted I would have paid them to take me.

I felt like Bette Davis when I saw my name on a dressing room door. The wardrobe director gave me my dress and a pair of black lace-up heels that looked like something my grandmother might have worn. I said, "If I'll wear these things, it proves I'll do anything to be in the movies."

I always imagined that everything about Hollywood and movie-making was very glamorous, but I can tell

124

you, having to be at the Griffin Holiday Inn at 6:30 every morning is not my idea of glamour. It hurts to get up that early and work until dark. There is a lot of standing around and waiting to see if they need you, but they do work hard.

Everyone has had a hand in making sure my ego hasn't gotten too big. My little granddaughter said "Grandmama, I didn't see you in the movie." I said, "That's the kindest thing anyone's said to me." My friend Liz Carpenter (who was Lady Bird Johnson's press secretary) keeps telling me I'm the Grandma Moses of the movie business.

Besides having a ball, and experiencing the thrill of seeing myself playing a movie role on television, I earned $1,384 for three days of work. I learned a little bit about the movie business, and I even gathered a few new recipes. On a movie set, "walking food" is served, because there is no way to get everybody seated at once for a meal. You have to be able to eat as you work. That's show biz, but it's also fairly typical of all busy people.

Following are several recipes good for on-the-go people.

ꕉWalking Breakfastsꕉ

(for movie stars and mortals who must eat on the run)

Country Fried Ham Biscuits
with Red Eye Gravy
Catch-Up Egg Sandwich
Sausage Pinwheels
Deviled Eggs with Bacon
Traveling Grits
Chocolate Waffle Sandwiches
with Strawberry Cream Cheese
Just Grab an Apple
Fruit on a Stick
Brenda's Breakfast Burritos
Cold Coca-Cola
Cold Orange Juice
Hot Coffee
Hot Chocolate

COUNTRY FRIED HAM BISCUITS WITH RED EYE GRAVY

Ingredients
for about 6 servings:

3 slices country ham, ¼ inch thick
¼ cup coffee (or water)
¼ tsp. sugar
6 large biscuits

Directions:

Fry ham on each side. Remove ham from drippings. Stir in coffee and sugar. Put ham back in gravy. Simmer till hot. Split biscuits open. Put in them ham and 1-2 tsp. gravy each.

Talmadge Tip:

If you can sit down to eat this breakfast, fill your plate with leftover biscuits and hot gravy — delicious!

CATCH-UP EGG SANDWICH

Ingredients for each sandwich:

1 egg
1 Tbl. bacon drippings
2 slices whole wheat toast
1 Tbl. catsup

Directions:

Fry egg in bacon drippings until the yolk is hard. Lightly douse with catsup. Place between two slices of hot toast. Slice on the diagonal. This sandwich won't drip on your tie as you drive to work.

SAUSAGE PINWHEELS

Ingredients for 2 dozen:

2½ cups biscuit mix
⅔ cup water
1 lb. raw Talmadge hot country sausage

Directions:

Make dough with biscuit mix and water. Roll ½ inch thick, about 7 by 12 inches. Spread raw sausage across center of dough. Roll into long "jelly roll." With string, cut ½-inch rounds from roll. Place on cookie sheet. Bake at 425° for 10-12 minutes. These may

be frozen after baking and re-
heated when ready to serve.
Serve with apple jelly.

DEVILED EGGS WITH BACON

Ingredients:

12 hard-cooked eggs
1 tsp. salt
½ tsp. prepared mustard
1 Tbl. vinegar
¼ tsp. paprika
mayonnaise to moisten
crumbled bacon bits

Directions:

Peel eggs. Cut in half. Remove
yolks. Mash yolks with all ingredients except mayonnaise and
bacon bits. Blend well. Moisten
with mayonnaise. Stuff halves.
Top with crisp, crumbled bacon
bits. Serve hot or cold.

TRAVELING GRITS

Ingredients for 12 mushrooms:

12 large mushrooms (about 1 lb.)
1 cup cooked grits
⅓ cup Parmesan cheese, grated
1 Tbl. chopped parsley
½ tsp. dry mustard
½ tsp. thyme
½ tsp. salt
dash pepper
chopped parsley for topping (optional)

Directions:

Remove stems from mushrooms. Finely chop enough stems to equal 1 cup. Combine chopped mushrooms with remaining ingredients. Mix well. Fill mushrooms caps. Top with additional chopped parsley, if desired. Place in shallow baking pan. Bake at 350° about 15 minutes.

CHOCOLATE WAFFLE SANDWICHES WITH STRAWBERRY CREAM CHEESE

Ingredients:

½ cup butter, melted
1 cup sugar
2 eggs
½ cup milk
1½ cups flour

2 tsp. baking powder
2 squares semisweet chocolate,
    melted
½ tsp. vanilla flavoring

Filling:
favorite brand of whipped cream
    cheese with strawberries
    (pineapple also works well)

Directions: Mix waffle ingredients until smooth. Bake in hot waffle iron. Spread whole waffle with filling. Cover with another waffle. Cut into sections. Serve warm.

JUST GRAB AN APPLE

Ingredients for each
serving: small apple
chunky peanut butter
currants or raisins

Directions: Wash and core apple to within ½ inch of bottom. Stuff cavity, alternating peanut butter and currants.

Talmadge Tip: Small apples are easier to hold and cut. Be sure not to core all the way through, or the stuffing will fall through the bottom.

FRUIT ON A STICK

Ingredients:

chunks of mixed fruit (apples, bananas, strawberries, grapes, pineapple)
wooden skewers or plastic coffee stirrers
lemonade concentrate

Directions:

Dip fruits that will turn dark into lemonade concentrate. Skewer on a stick and walk out the door munching.

BRENDA'S BREAKFAST BURRITOS

Ingredients for each serving:

1 Tbl. margarine
1 10-inch flour or corn tortilla
¼ cup Cheddar cheese, grated
2 strips bacon, cooked and crumbled *or* 1-2 oz. Talmadge hot country sausage, cooked and crumbled
1 egg, scrambled
prepared taco sauce, hot or mild
optional: diced tomatoes, onion; shredded lettuce

Directions:

Cook tortilla in hot margarine 30 seconds. Flip. Sprinkle with remaining ingredients. When cheese melts, roll tortilla into cylinder shape (use tongs). Wrap with wax paper. Serve hot.

Talmadge Tip:

Leave the wax paper wrapped around the burrito. Peel it down as you eat. This keeps the filling and sauce from dripping out. Be careful not to overfill the tortilla. Although delicious, it is more difficult to manage.

THE POLITICS OF FINE FOOD

I often say that my life has been up and down, but it has never been boring. A long time ago, I decided I couldn't be content sitting at my sewing box watching the world go by. I enjoy homey things like cooking and needlepointing, and I still spend a lot of time doing those things. But I wouldn't trade the challenges I've had outside my home for anything in the world. I count my experiences as businesswoman, cookbook writer, "movie star," and politician among the most rewarding of those challenges.

I wasn't successful in politics in that I lost my election for the U.S. Congress in 1978, but I'm glad I ran. It was something I needed to try, because it was in my blood. I was born into politics and have been on the sidelines of one campaign or another most of my life.

My daddy was the mayor of Ashburn, Georgia, and my granddaddy was in the state senate. When I was twenty-four years old, my former husband was elected governor. Later I went to Washington as a senator's wife.

The very first social experience I remember was a political barbecue. There have been hundreds more. But I love the atmosphere of a political party. People come together with a common bond—their support for a candidate, their belief in their party, and many times their friendship.

In the South, one of the best political parties is the

Pig Pickin'. I had the privilege of having a Pig Pickin' here during the Carter campaign when the women in the Democratic Party decided they wanted to honor Rosalynn Carter and Joan Mondale. We were known as the Committee of 51.3%. Men kept saying. "What in the world is the Committee of 51.3%?" We would tell them proudly, "The women, and it's about time you knew it."

At that pig pickin' we served the now famous "Fritz's Grits," which was my cheese grits named for Fritz Mondale, and seven barbecued pigs.

The mood was one of enthusiasm, because we all felt we were on the way to victory, and of course, we were right.

But, losing can be fun, too. Last year, I participated in a Losers party, sponsored by a group of my friends who get together once a month for dinner. This group, made up of food writers, consultants and just plain food lovers, concocts a theme each month for a party. We each bring a dish that fits the theme. (One May we had a Romantic May Night, and sometimes we celebrate a member's birthday.) After the last gubernatorial race, we had the First Quadrennial Crow Fest. We sent invitations entitled "Defeat is an Orphan" to everyone who ran. Most of them came, and after they had feasted on Crow Balls and Lame Duck Pâté, you would have thought they had won the election.

Another fun political party I used to attend was the quail supper sponsored each year by the Lowndes County delegation to the Georgia General Assembly. Judge Harley Langdale began the tradition years ago by bringing quail and sometimes dove up from his farm, and then fixing supper for friends. Over the years the guest list grew to include the whole legislature, and the

Ulysses S. Grunt attends many of my political parties

party was moved to the old Dinkler Hotel. The quails and doves were the main course, but as you might expect, there also was a lot of bull at these parties.

Southern-Style Crow Fest

(for campaign losers and lamenters)

Old Crow on Ice
Sacked Wine
Lame Duck Pâté on Ceded Wafers
Baloney
Crow Balls
Dark Horse Dip and Bitters
Beat Salad
Waterloo Celery with Old Goat Cheese
Sour Grapes Salad
Cooked Goose in
Whipped Potato Cups
Depressed Duck
Agony of deFeet
Ill Wind Beans   Stewed Tomatoes
Beaten Biscuits
Hat in the Ring Cake
Bar the Nuts

OLD CROW ON ICE

Old Crow bourbon on crushed ice

SACKED WINE

Dry sack sherry on ice or "straight up"

LAME DUCK PÂTÉ ON CEDED WAFERS

Ingredients:

½ lb. chicken livers
2 hard-cooked eggs
3 Tbl. sour cream or mayonnaise
salt
pepper
1 small onion, chopped
watercress
sesame seed crackers

Directions:

Simmer livers in water to cover until just done. Drain. In blender, blend all ingredients (except watercress and crackers) at medium speed until smooth. Pack into small mold. Chill. Unmold onto bed of fresh watercress. Serve on Ceded Wafers (sesame seed crackers).

BALONEY

Ingredients:

bologna, sliced wafer-thin
pickle spears, split in half length-
wise
fancy toothpicks

Directions:

Wrap bologna around pickle
strips. Fasten with toothpicks.
Arrange on serving tray.

CROW BALLS

Ingredients:

melon balls (made from canta-
loupe, watermelon, honey-
dew melon, etc.)
shaved baked Talmadge ham
fancy toothpicks

Directions:

Wrap shaved ham around
melon balls. Fasten with fancy
toothpicks.

DARK HORSE DIP AND BITTERS

Ingredients:

12 hard-cooked eggs
1½ Tbl. liquid smoke
1 Tbl. wine vinegar
2 tsp. brown mustard
2 tsp. Worcestershire sauce
4 drops Tabasco sauce

1 tsp. onion salt
1 tsp. salt
¼ tsp. pepper
1 cup mayonnaise
few drops bitters

Directions: Use food processor or blender to finely grate eggs and mix ingredients. Blend until smooth. Chill. Serve with crackers, chips, raw broccoli, squash, cauliflower, turnip slices, etc.

BEAT SALAD

Ingredients: 1 bunch beets (at least 1 lb.)
½ cup sugar
2 cups white vinegar
Bibb lettuce
mayonnaise
few drops beet marinade
dried chervil for garnish

Directions: Boil beets until tender. Peel, slice. Dissolve sugar in vinegar. Pour over beets. Refrigerate overnight. Lay sliced beets over lettuce. Mix mayonnaise with marinade. Dollop on salad. Garnish with dried chervil.

Talmadge Tip: Canned, pickled beets may be used.

WATERLOO CELERY WITH OLD GOAT CHEESE

Ingredients: Roquefort cheese
sour cream
garlic salt
pepper
celery stalks, cut into 2½-inch
   lengths

Directions: Mix equal parts of Roquefort
cheese and sour cream. Season
with garlic salt and pepper. Fill
celery stalks.

SOUR GRAPES SALAD

Ingredients: ½ cup seedless grapes, sliced in
   halves
2 cups grapefruit sections
2 Tbl. white wine
2 Tbl. bottled French dressing
endive
sour cream
paprika

Directions: Marinate grapes and grapefruit
in wine and French dressing for
1-3 hours. Arrange on bed of
endive. Garnish with sour cream
and paprika.

COOKED GOOSE

Ingredients:

4 cups sliced roast goose (or chicken)
2 Tbl. lemon juice
2 Tbl. Worcestershire sauce
2 cups goose (or chicken) gravy
12 ripe olives, sliced
½ cup sherry
Whipped Potato Cups

Directions:

Simmer all ingredients except sherry and Whipped Potato Cups. Add sherry. Pour into serving bowl. Let guests spoon into Whipped Potato Cups.

WHIPPED POTATO CUPS

Ingredients for 8-12 servings:

butter
8 cups mashed potatoes (cold or hot)
paprika

Directions:

Fill large, buttered muffin tins or pyrex cups with mashed potato. Make hollows in the potatoes with the bottom of a small glass. Sprinkle with paprika. Heat in 350° oven until slightly brown. Slip out carefully onto serving plate. Let guests serve themselves, spooning Cooked Goose into the Whipped Potato Cups.

DEPRESSED DUCK

Ingredients:

2 ducks
4 small onions, peeled
Worcestershire sauce
flour
salt
pepper
4 strips bacon

Directions:

Clean and dry ducks. Put 2 whole onions inside each duck. Sprinkle with Worcestershire

144

sauce, flour, salt, and pepper. Place in self-basting roaster. Lay two strips of bacon across each bird. Fasten with toothpicks. Cover bottom of roaster with water. Cover. Roast at 350° about 1¾ hours, depending on the size of ducks. Remove cover and bake 20 minutes to brown skin. Slice and serve at the buffet table.

AGONY OF DEFEET

Ingredients:
cured pigs' feet
water for cooking
vinegar
bay leaves
allspice

Directions:
Simmer cured feet in water until tender. Drain. Cover with vinegar and spices. Chill. May be kept in the vinegar for 3 weeks.

Talmadge Tip:
Estimated serving only 1 per 25 guests, as very few people like to participate in the agony of defeet.

ILL WIND BEANS

Ingredients for 6-12 servings:	6 cups cooked green beans 3 slices bacon, cooked crisp
Directions:	Fill serving bowl with hot, cooked beans. Finely crumble crisp bacon on top to garnish.

STEWED TOMATOES

Ingredients:	1 Tbl. bacon drippings 1 lb. okra, cut in pieces (or 1 10-oz. package frozen okra) 4 fresh tomatoes, chopped (or 1 16-oz. can tomatoes) 1 onion, chopped 1 tsp. Worcestershire sauce salt pepper ½ tsp. sugar
Directions:	Sauté okra in bacon drippings. Add remaining ingredients. Cook until onion is tender. Do not add water.

BEATEN BISCUITS

Ingredients for 90 party-sized biscuits:	6 cups flour, sifted and measured 1 tsp. salt

1 Tbl. sugar
1 tsp. baking powder
1 cup cold lard or shortening
½ cup cold milk
½ cup ice water

Directions:

Preheat oven to 375°. Using a food processor, mix dry ingredients. Cut in the lard until the lumps are out. Add milk and water. Begin kneading into a ball. If dry or crumbly, add more milk. Continue kneading in the food processor for 2 minutes, until dough is smooth and marbled. Remove from processor. Roll dought ½ inch thick. Cut in 1¼-inch party-sized rounds. Place on a baking sheet. Pierce with a fork, making 2 parallel sets of holes in the biscuit all the way to the pan. Keep rolling scraps and making more biscuits. Place in the preheated oven. Turn down to 350°. Bake for 30 minutes. Do not brown. Serve hot or cold. They will keep for weeks in a tight tin or in the freezer.

Talmadge Tip:

Beaten biscuits are a different kind of biscuit. They are firm, not light, more like a thick cracker. Bland, they are the perfect foil for salty country ham.

HAT IN THE RING CAKE

Ingredients:

8 eggs whites
1 cup butter
2 cups sugar
4 cups flour
2 heaping tsp. baking powder
pinch salt
1 cup milk
1 tsp. vanilla flavoring
Filling:
8 egg yolks
1 cup sugar
¼ cup butter, melted
1 cup raisins
1 cup pecans
2 oz. wine or bourbon whiskey
1 tsp. vanilla flavoring
Frosting:
2 cups sugar
½ cup water
2-3 Tbl. white corn syrup
2 egg whites

Directions:

Beat egg whites until stiff. Set aside. Combine butter, sugar, flour, baking powder, and salt. Add milk and vanilla flavoring. Fold in egg whites. Grease and flour 9-inch cake pans. Fill pans ⅔ full. Bake at 350° for 45 minutes. Cool. Remove from pans.

Make filling: Beat egg yolks. Add remaining filling ingredients. Cook in double boiler until thick. Spread between the cake layers.

Make frosting: Combine all frosting ingredients except egg whites. Cook until mixture forms a soft ball in cold water. Beat egg whites until stiff. Fold in. Spread over top and sides of cake while still warm.

Talmadge Tip: Men are especially fond of this cake. I guess it is because of the wine or bourbon in the filling.

BAR THE NUTS

Ingredients:
⅓ cup sugar
⅓ cup brown sugar
1 cup flour
1 cup quick-cooking oats, un-cooked
⅓ cup crunchy peanut butter
1 egg
½ tsp. vanilla flavoring
½ cup butter, melted

Directions:
Combine sugars, flour, and oatmeal. Cut in peanut butter. Add remaining ingredients. Mix well. Press into a greased 9-by-12-inch pan. Bake at 350° for 15-20 minutes. Cut into bars and serve.

Georgia Legislators' Bird Dinner

(for hawks and doves and other birds of a feather)

*Doves with Gravy on
Thick Toast*

Capitol Quail

Wild Rice

Orator's Onions in Foil

Corn Sticks

*Senate Salad with
House Dressing*

Baked Apples

Fried Up Okra

Greenhorn Beans with Small Potatoes

Filibuster Pie

Coffee with Cream and Sugar

DOVES WITH GRAVY

Ingredients: doves, fully cleaned
water
flour
butter
salt
pepper
chicken stock (optional)

Directions: Cook doves in water to cover until meat practically falls off the bones. Remove doves. Use stock and flour to make medium-thick gravy (2 Tbl. flour per cup of stock). Season with butter, salt, and pepper. Use chicken stock, if more gravy is needed. To serve, place dove on slice of Thick Toast. Cover with gravy.

THICK TOAST

Ingredients: loaves of crisp French bread
melted butter
garlic salt

Directions: Slice bread in 1½-inch pieces. Pour melted butter over bread. Sprinkle with garlic salt. Bake uncovered at 375°, until crisp and browned.

CAPITOL QUAIL

Ingredients: frozen quail
                   salt water
                   pepper
                   butter
                   sherry or white wine

Directions: Thaw quail in salt water. Sprin-
                   kle with pepper. Melt butter in
                   skillet. Brown birds. Place birds in
                   casserole. Add remaining ingre-
                   dients to skillet. Make about ½
                   inch deep with wine. Heat
                   thoroughly. Pour over birds in
                   casserole. Cover. Bake at 350° for
                   about 30-45 minutes, or until
                   done. Serve with Wild Rice.

WILD RICE

Ingredients: 2 cups wild rice, uncooked
                   chicken broth
                   ½ cup celery, chopped
                   salt
                   pepper

Directions: Cook wild rice according to
                   package directions, substituting
                   chicken broth for water. Add
                   celery, salt, and pepper 15 min-
                   utes before end of cooking time.

152

ORATOR'S ONIONS IN FOIL

Ingredients:

Vidalia onions
Worcestershire Sauce
salt
pepper
butter, cut in pats

Directions:

Peel onions. Core out small amount of middle. Fill with remaining ingredients. Wrap in foil. Bake at 325° for 40 minutes.

CORN STICKS

Ingredients for 20 small muffins:

¾ cup flour
2½ tsp. baking powder
1 Tbl. sugar
½ tsp. salt
1¼ cups cornmeal
1 egg, slightly beaten
2 Tbl. butter, melted
1 cup buttermilk

Directions:

Grease muffin tins. Place in oven to heat. Sift dry ingredients together. Add egg, butter, and buttermilk. Pour into hot muffin tins. Bake at 425° for 20-25 minutes.

SENATE SALAD

Ingredients:

endive
lettuce
tomatoes
cucumbers
radishes

Directions:

Make tossed salad from ingredients. Serve with House Dressing.

HOUSE DRESSING

Ingredients:

bottled Thousand Island dressing
bottled French dressing
bacon bits
garlic croutons

Directions:

Mix equal amounts of dressings. Add bacon bits to taste. Garnish salad with garlic croutons.

BAKED APPLES

Ingredients:

12 red apples, unpeeled
1 cup fresh cranberries
¼ tsp. salt
1 cup water
sugar to taste

Directions:

Core and thickly slice apples. Mix all ingredients in large casserole. Bake at 350° until apples are soft, but not mushy.

FRIED UP OKRA

Ingredients:

1 lb. okra
¼ cup cornmeal
¼ cup flour
1 tsp. salt
1 cup peanut or vegetable oil, or
    melted shortening
pepper

Directions:

Rinse the okra. Remove the caps. Cut into ¼-inch pieces. Mix cornmeal, flour, and salt. Toss the okra with mixture. Spread out for a few minutes to dry. Toss again. Fill skillet halfway with oil. Heat to sizzling. Add okra. Leave enough room to turn. Fry until lightly browned, turning only to prevent burning. Add salt and pepper while still hot.

Talmadge Tip:

Okra pods should be small, not much bigger than the size of your little finger. When they are any larger, or old, their milky substance dilutes the fat and you wind up with a mess. Okra should be eaten right away.

GREENHORN BEANS WITH SMALL POTATOES

Ingredients:

2½ lbs. green beans, broken into 1-inch pieces
¼ lb. fatback
1 tsp. salt
2 cups water
12 small, new potatoes, unpeeled and scrubbed

Directions:

Combine all ingredients except potatoes in a heavy Dutch oven. Bring to a boil. Cover. Reduce heat. Cook 30 minutes. Add potatoes. Cover. Cook for 30 minutes or until tender.

FILIBUSTER PIE

Ingredients:

4 oz. semisweet chocolate, melted
½ cup brown sugar
4 eggs
½ cup light corn syrup
⅔ cup bourbon whiskey
1 Tbl. molasses
1 tsp. salt
2 cups pecan halves
1 9-inch, unbaked pie shell

Directions:

With electric mixer, beat chocolate and sugar until fluffy. Beat in remaining ingredients, except pecans and pie shell. Fold in pecans. Pour into pie shell. Bake 10 minutes at 450°. Lower heat to 325°. Bake 30 minutes more, or until set.

I hope you've enjoyed your visit to Lovejoy Plantation, and I hope you will enjoy trying many of my favorite recipes in this book. Good friends and good food — that's the basis of Southern hospitality.

Happy cooking!

Betty Talmadge

INDEX

Agony of deFeet 138, 145
Ambrosia: Fruits of the Gods 59, 68
APPETIZERS
  Baloney 138, 140
  Celery Stalks 59
  Cheese Wafers 41, 47
  Cottage Dill Bread 41, 44-45
  Crow Balls 138, 140
  Dark Horse Dip and Bitters 138, 140-141
  Deviled Eggs with Bacon 126, 129
  Garden Tomato Sandwiches 41, 42-43
  Lame Duck Pâté on Ceded Wafers 138, 139
  Miniature Ham Biscuits 70, 75
  Plantation Vegetables Relish Tray 6, 8-9
  Ringin'-in-the-New-Year Relishes 76, 77
  Sausage Minié Balls 6, 8
  Sausage Pinwheels 126, 128-129
  Stuffed Green Olives 59
  Tara Toasted Pecans 6, 7
  Traveling Grits 126, 130
  Waterloo Celery with Old Goat Cheese 138, 142
Apples (see Fruits)
Aunt Pittypat's Homemade Peach Ice Cream 6, 14

Back Yard Corn on the Cob 94, 98
Baked Apples 150, 155
Baloney 138, 140
Bar the Nuts 138, 149
BARBECUE
  Barbecued Spareribs 76, 78
  Blazin' Barbecue Sauce 23, 28, 76
  John Wilkes' Pit-Roasted Pig 23, 26-27
  Roasted Suckling Pig 23, 24-25
Barbecued Spareribs 76, 78
Beans (see Vegetables)
Beer in the Bucket 23, 24
Beat Salad 138, 141
Beaten Biscuits 138, 146-147
Beets (see Beat Salad)
Belle Watling's Wicked Mint Julep 6, 7

Bentley's Homemade Bran Bread 76, 84
BEVERAGES
  Beer in the Bucket 23, 24
  Belle Watling's Wicked Mint Julep 6, 7
  Champagne Peach Punch 41, 42
  Company's Comin' Egg Nog 70, 71
  Hot Pot Likker 76, 77
  Old Crow on Ice 138, 139
  Sacked Wine 138, 139
  Strawberry Smoothies 94, 100
Billy T. Sherman's Chocolate Glutton Pie 94, 99
Biscuits (see Breads)
Black-Eyed Peas with Hog Jowl 76, 79
Blazin' Barbecue Sauce 23, 28, 76
Blueberry Pie (see Virginia Callaway's Blueberry Pie)
Bologna (see Baloney)
Brandy Baked Thanksgiving Ham 59, 60-61
BREADS
  BISCUITS
    Beaten Biscuits 138, 146-147
    Rhett Butler's Biscuits 6, 13
  CORNBREADS
    'Cile's Corn Pones 76, 85
    Corn Sticks 150, 153
    Hoecakes 105, 166
    Mammy's Cracklin Cornbread 23, 33
    Ruff's Painted Hush Puppies 94, 97
  GRITS
    Traveling Grits 126, 130
    True Grits à la Robert E. Lee 6, 12-13
  MISCELLANEOUS BREADS
    Bentley's Homemade Bran Bread 76, 84
    Cheese Wafers 41, 47
    Cottage Dill Bread 41, 44-45
    Criss-Cross Yeast Rolls 59, 66
    Dixie Breaking Bread 23, 32
    Sally Lunn Bread (see Toasted Sally Lunn Bread)
    Thick Toast 150, 151

160

MISCELLANEOUS BREADS, *Cont.*
 Toasted Sally Lunn Bread 41, 48
 Wild Rice 150, 152
Brenda's Breakfast Burritos 126, 132-
 133
BRUNSWICK STEW
 Jimmy's Brunswick Stew 105, 113
 Twelve Oaks Brunswick Stew 23, 29
Burritos (*see* Brenda's Breakfast Burri-
 tos)

Cabbage (*see* Old South Cabbage Slaw)
Cakes (*see* Desserts)
Candied Sweet Potatoes (*see* Ocilla
 Candied Sweet Potatoes)
Capitol Quail 150, 152
Carrots (*see* Scarlett's Carrots)
Catch-Up Egg Sandwich 126, 128
Celery Stalks 59
Champagne Peach Punch 41, 42
Charlotte Russe 59, 68-69
Charlotte's Peanut Butter Pie 23, 34-35
CHEESE
 Cheese Wafers 41, 47
 Chocolate Waffle Sandwich with
  Strawberry Cream Cheese 126,
  130-131
 True Grits à la Robert E. Lee 6, 12-13
 Waterloo Celery with Old Goat
  Cheese 138, 142
Cheese Wafers 41, 47
Chick 'n' Lily Salad 41, 46
Chicken (*see* Poultry)
Chitlins 105, 108-109
Chitterlings (*see* Chitlins)
CHOCOLATE
 Billy T. Sherman's Chocolate Glut-
  ton Pie 94, 99
 Chocolate Waffle Sandwiches with
  Strawberry Cream Cheese 126,
  130-131
 Filibuster Pie 150, 158
 Gorp by Sam B. 94, 100
Chocolate Waffle Sandwiches with
 Strawberry Cream Cheese 126, 130-
 131
Christmas Coconut Cake 70, 74
'Cile's Corn Pones 76, 85
City-Style Green Peas 59, 63
Cole Slaw (*see* Old South Cabbage
 Slaw)
Collards (*see* Vegetables)

Company's Comin' Egg Nog 70, 71
Confederate Butter Balls 41, 50
Confederate Cucumber Mousse and
 Tomatoes 6, 11
Cooked Goose 138, 143
Cookies (*see* Desserts)
Corn (*see* Back Yard Corn on the Cob)
Cornbread (*see* Breads)
Corn Dogs (*see* Pigs on a Stick)
Corn Pones (*see* 'Cile's Corn Pones)
Corn Sticks 150, 153
Cottage Dill Bread 41, 44-45
Country Cracklin's 105, 107
Country Fried Ham Biscuits with Red
 Eye Gravy 126, 127
Cracklings (*see* Country Cracklins)
Crackling Cornbread (*see* Mammy's
 Cracklin Cornbread)
Cranberry Salad 59, 60
Criss-Cross Yeast Rolls 59, 66
Crisp Atlanta Potatoes 23, 30-31
Crow Balls 138, 140
Cucumbers (*see* Vegetables)

Dark Horse Dip and Bitters 138, 140-
 141
Depressed Duck 138, 144-145
DESSERTS
 CAKES
  Christmas Coconut Cake 70, 74
  Hat in the Ring Cake 138, 148-149
  Lane Cake (*see* Hat in the Ring
   Cake)
  Louise Hastings' Fruitcake 70, 72-
   73
 COOKIES
  Confederate Butter Balls 41, 50
  Lovejoy Lace Cookies 6, 14-15
  Petite Pecan Tassies 41, 51
  Rainbow Sugar Cookies 94, 98-99
 ICE CREAMS
  Aunt Pittypat's Homemade Peach
   Ice Cream 6, 14
  Ice Cream Cones 94
  Miss Prissy's Sherried Fig Ice
   Cream 41, 50
 MISCELLANEOUS DESSERTS
  Ambrosia: Fruits of the Gods 59,
   68
  Bar the Nuts 138, 149
  Charlotte Russe 59, 68-69
  Chocolate Waffle Sandwiches

with Strawberry Cream Cheese 126, 130-131
Gorp by Sam B. 94, 100
Nesselrode Pudding 70, 72
Southern Gingerbread with Caramel Sauce 76, 86
Strawberry Smoothies 94, 100
Tipsy Tom 23, 36
PIES
    Billy T. Sherman's Chocolate Glutton Pie 94, 99
    Charlotte's Peanut Butter Pie 23, 34-35
    Filibuster Pie 150, 158
    Little Lady Lemon Pies 41, 52-53
    Petite Pecan Tassies 41, 51
    Pumpkin-Pecan Pie 59, 67
    Virginia Callaway's Blueberry Pie 23, 35
Deviled Eggs with Bacon 126, 129
Dip (see Dark Horse Dip and Bitters)
Dixie Breaking Bread 23, 32
Doves with Gravy 150, 151
Duck (see Depressed Duck)

EGGS
    Catch-Up Egg Sandwich 126, 128
    Company's Comin' Egg Nog 70, 71
    Dark Horse Dip and Bitters 138, 140-141
    Deviled Eggs with Bacon 126, 129

Ferrol's Vegetable Garden Soup 105, 117
Filibuster Pie 150, 158
Fried Up Okra 150, 156
Fruit on a Stick 126, 132
Fruitcake (see Louise Hastings' Fruitcake)

FRUITS
    APPLES
        Baked Apples 150, 155
        Just Grab an Apple 126, 131
    MELONS
        Chick 'n' Lily Salad 41, 46
    Crow Balls 138, 140
    MISCELLANEOUS FRUITS
        Ambrosia: Fruits of the Gods 59, 68
        Fruit on a Stick 126, 132
        Miss Prissy's Sherried Fig Ice

Cream 41, 50
Sour Grapes Salad 138, 142
Spicey Plums 41, 49
Strawberry Smoothies 94, 100
Watermelon Slices 94
PEACHES
    Aunt Pittypat's Homemade Peach Ice Cream 6, 14
    Champagne Peach Punch 41, 42
    Plumb Pickled Peaches 23, 32
    Tipsy Peaches 41, 49

Garden Tomato Sandwiches 41, 42-43
Georgia Legislators' Bird Dinner 150
Gingerbread (see Southern Gingerbread with Caramel Sauce)
Goose (see Cooked Goose)
Gorp by Sam B. 94, 100
Grandma Shingler's Liver Puddin' 105, 109
Grandma Shingler's Scalloped Oysters 59, 62
Grapes (see Sour Grapes Salad)
GRAVIES
    Dove Gravy 150, 151
    Red Eye Gravy 126, 127
Green and Red Pepper Jelly 76, 82-83
Greenback Collards 76, 80
Greenhorn Beans with Small Potatoes 150, 157
Green Peas (see City-Style Green Peas)
Grits (see Breads)

Ham (see Pork)
Hastings, Louise Fruitcake (see Louise Hastings' Fruitcake)
Hat in the Ring Cake 138, 148-149
Head Cheese Loaf 105, 110
Hen Legs in Bean Beds 94, 96-97
Hoecakes 105, 116
Honeysuckle Luncheon at Tara 41
Horseback Sauce 94, 96
Hot Country Farm Sausage 105, 112-113
Hot Dogs (see Pigs on a Stick)
Hot Pot Likker 76, 77
House Dressing 150, 154
Hush Puppies (see Ruff's Painted Hush Puppies)

Ice Cream Cones 94

162

Ice Creams (see Desserts)
Ill Wind Beans 138, 146

JELLIES
Green and Red Pepper Jelly 76, 82-83
Old-Fashioned Quincedonia Preserves 105, 119
Pomegranate Jelly 105, 118
Tomato Marmalade 76, 82
Jimmy's Brunswick Stew 105, 113
John Wilkes' Pit-Roasted Pig 23, 26-27
Just Grab an Apple 126, 131

Kids' Things 94

Lame Duck Pâté on Ceded Wafers 138, 139
Lane Cake (see Hat in the Ring Cake)
Lemon Pie (see Little Lady Lemon Pies)
Little Lady Lemon Pies 41, 52-53
LIVER
Grandma Shingler's Liver Puddin' 105, 109
Lame Duck Pâté on Ceded Wafers 138, 139
Liver Sausage 105, 111
Liver Pudding (see Grandma Shingler's Liver Puddin')
Liver Sausage 105, 111
Louise Hastings' Fruitcake 70, 72-73
Lovejoy Lace Cookies 6, 14-15
Lovejoy Plantation Christmas 70
Lovejoy Plantation Magnolia Barbecue 23

A Magnolia Supper at Lovejoy 6
Mammy's Cracklin Cornbread 23, 33
Melanie's Marinated Cucumbers 23, 31
MENUS
Georgia Legislators' Bird Dinner 150
Honeysuckle Luncheon at Tara 41
Kids' Things 94
Lovejoy Plantation Christmas 70
Lovejoy Plantation Magnolia Barbecue 23
A Magnolia Supper at Lovejoy 6
New Years' Day Supper 76
Southern-Style Crow Fest 138
Thanksgiving Talmadge Style 59
Trotters, Tales, and Other Wild Weeds 105
Walking Breakfasts 126

Mild Country Farm Sausage 105, 112
Miniature Ham Biscuits 70, 75
Mint Julep (see Belle Watling's Wicked Mint Julep)
Miss Prissy's Sherried Fig Ice Cream 41, 50
Mousse (see Confederate Cucumber Mousse and Tomatoes)
Mustard Sauce (see Sweet-Hot Mustard Sauce)

Nesselrode Pudding 70, 72
New Year's Day Supper 76

Ocilla Candied Sweet Potatoes 59, 64
Okra (see Fried Up Okra)
Old Crow on Ice 138, 139
Old-Fashioned Quincedonia Preserves 105, 119
Old South Cabbage Slaw 23, 30
Onions (see Orator's Onions in Foil)
Opossum (see Roast 'Possum)
Orator's Onions in Foil 150, 153

Pâté (see Lame Duck Pâté on Ceded Wafers)
Peaches (see Fruits)
Pecans (see Tara Toasted Pecans)
Peppers (see Green and Red Pepper Jelly)
Petite Pecan Tassies 41, 51
Pies (see Desserts)
Pigs' Feet (see Pork)
Pigs on a Stick 94, 95
Plantation Vegetables Relish Tray 6, 8-9
Plumb Pickled Peaches 23, 32
Plums (see Spicey Plums)
Poke Salad (see Vegetables)
Poke Salad Sambo 105, 114
Poke Salit Helen 105, 115
Pomegranate Jelly 105, 118
PORK
HAM
Brandy Baked Thanksgiving Ham 59, 60-61
Country Fried Ham Biscuits with Red Eye Gravy 126, 127
Talmadge Country Ham 6, 9
MISCELLANEOUS
Chitlins 105, 108-109
Chitterlings (see Chitlins)

163

Country Cracklins 105, 107
Grandma Shingler's Liver Puddin' 105, 109
Head Cheese Loaf 105, 110
Salt Pork, Fried (*see* Sawmill Chicken)
Sawmill Chicken 105, 106-107
PIG'S FEET
    Agony of deFeet 138, 145
    Trotters, Pickled 105, 106
SAUSAGE
    Hot Country Farm Sausage 105, 112-113
    Liver Sausage 105, 111
    Mild Country Farm Sausage 105, 112
    Sausage Minié Balls 6, 8
    Sausage Pinwheels 126, 128-129
WHOLE PIG
    John Wilkes' Pit-Roasted Pig 23, 26-27
    Roasted Suckling Pig 23, 24-25
Possum (*see* Roast 'Possum)
Potatoes (*see* Vegetables)
POULTRY
CHICKEN
    Chick 'n' Lily Salad 41, 46
    Cooked Goose 138, 143
    Hen Legs in Bean Beds 94, 96-97
    Lame Duck Pâté on Ceded Wafers 138, 139
    Southern Fried Chicken 6, 10
MISCELLANEOUS
    Capitol Quail 150, 152
    Cooked Goose 138, 143
    Depressed Duck 138, 144-145
    Doves with Gravy 150, 151
Pudding (*see* Nesselrode Pudding)
Pumpkin-Pecan Pie 59, 67

Quail (*see* Capitol Quail)

Rainbow Sugar Cookies 94, 98-99
Red Eye Gravy (*see* Country Fried Ham Biscuits with Red Eye Gravy)
Refrigerator Green Tomato Pickles 59, 64-65
RELISHES
    Green and Red Pepper Jelly 76, 82-83
    Melanie's Marinated Cucumbers 23, 31

Plantation Vegetables Relish Tray 6, 8-9
Plumb Pickled Peaches 23, 32
Refrigerator Green Tomato Pickles 59, 64-65
Ringin'-in-the-New-Year Relishes 76, 77
Stuffed Green Olives 59
Rhett Butler's Biscuits 6, 13
Rice (*see* Wild Rice)
Ringin'-in-the-New-Year Relishes 76, 77
Roast 'Possum 105, 120-121
Roasted Suckling Pig 23, 24-25
Ruff's Painted Hush Puppies 94, 97
Rutabaga Turnips 76, 80-81

Sacked Wine 138, 139
SALADS
    Beat Salad 138, 141
    Chick 'n' Lily Salad 41, 46
    Cranberry Salad 59, 60
    Deviled Eggs with Bacon 126, 129
    Old South Cabbage Slaw 23, 30
    Senate Salad 150, 154
Salad Dressing (*see* House Dressing)
Sally Lunn Bread (*see* Toasted Sally Lunn Bread)
Salt Pork, Fried (*see* Sawmill Chicken)
SANDWICHES
    Catch-Up Egg Sandwich 126, 128
    Chocolate Waffle Sandwiches with Strawberry Cream Cheese 126, 130-131
    Country Fried Ham Biscuits with Red Eye Gravy 126, 127
    Garden Tomato Sandwiches 41, 42-43
SAUCES
    Blazin' Barbecue Sauce 23, 28, 76
    Caramel Sauce 76, 86
    Dark Horse Dip and Bitters 138, 140-141
    Ham Glaze (Brandy Baked Thanksgiving Ham) 59, 60-61
    Horseback Sauce 94, 96
    Sweet-Hot Mustard Sauce 70, 75
Sausage (*see* Pork)
Sausage Minié Balls 6, 8
Sausage Pinwheels 126, 128-29
Sawmill Chicken 105, 106-107
Scarlett's Carrots 6, 12

Seafood (*see* Grandma Shingler's Scalloped Oysters)
Senate Salad 150, 154
SOUPS
Ferrol's Vegetable Garden Soup 105, 117
Jimmy's Brunswick Stew 105, 113
Twelve Oaks Brunswick Stew 23, 29
Sour Grapes Salad 138, 142
Southern Fried Chicken 6, 10
Southern Gingerbread with Caramel Sauce 76, 86
Southern-Style Crow Fest 138
Spareribs (*see* Barbecued Spareribs)
Spicey Plums 41, 49
Stew (*see* Soups)
Stewed Tomatoes 138, 146
Strawberries (*see* Strawberry Smoothies)
Strawberry Smoothies 94, 100
Stuffed Green Olives 59
Sweet-Hot Mustard Sauce 70, 75
Sweet Potatoes (*see* Ocilla Candied Sweet Potatoes)

Talmadge Country Ham 6, 9
Tara Toasted Pecans, 6, 7
Thanksgiving Talmadge Style 59
Thick Toast 150, 151
Tipsy Peaches 41, 49
Tipsy Tom 23, 36
Toasted Sally Lunn Bread 41, 48
Tomato Marmalade 76, 82
Tomatoes (*see* Vegetables)
Traveling Grits 126, 130
Trotters, Pickled 105, 106
Trotters, Tales, and Other Wild Weeds 105
True Grits à la Robert E. Lee 6, 12-13
Twelve Oaks Brunswick Stew 23, 29
Turnip Greens with Fatback 59, 63
Turnips (*see* Vegetables)

VEGETABLES
BEANS
Greenhorn Beans with Small Potatoes 150, 157
Ill Wind Beans 138, 146
COLLARDS
Greenback Collards 76, 80

Hot Pot Likker 76, 77
CUCUMBERS
Confederate Cucumber Mousse and Tomatoes 6, 11
Melanie's Marinated Cucumbers 23, 31
MISCELLANEOUS VEGETABLES
Back Yard Corn on the Cob 94, 98
Beat Salad 138, 141
Celery Stalks 59
Ferrol's Vegetable Garden Soup 105, 117
Fried Up Okra 150, 156
Ocilla Candied Sweet Potatoes 59, 64
Orator's Onions in Foil 150, 153
Rutabaga Turnips 76, 80-81
Scarlett's Carrots 6, 12
PEAS
Black-Eyed Peas with Hog Jowl 76, 79
City-Style Green Peas 59, 63
POKE SALAD
Poke Salad Sambo 105, 114
Poke Salit Helen 105, 115
POTATOES
Crisp Atlanta Potatoes 23, 30-31
Whipped Potato Cups 138, 144
RELISHES
Green and Red Pepper Jelly 76, 82-83
Melanie's Marinated Cucumbers 23, 31
Plantation Vegetables Relish Tray 6, 8-9
Refrigerator Green Tomato Pickles 59, 64-65
Ringin'-in-the-New-Year Relishes 76, 77
Stuffed Green Olives 59
SALADS
Beat Salad 138, 141
Old South Cabbage Slaw 23, 30
Senate Salad 150, 154
TOMATOES
Garden Tomato Sandwiches 41, 42-43
Refrigerator Green Tomato Pickles 59, 64-65
Stewed Tomatoes 138, 146
Tomato Marmalade 76, 82

TURNIPS
  Rutabaga Turnips 76, 80-81
  Turnip Greens with Fatback 59, 63

Virginia Callaway's Blueberry Pie 23, 35

Waffles (see Chocolate Waffle Sandwiches with Strawberry Cream Cheese)

Walking Breakfasts 126
Waterloo Celery with Old Goat Cheese 138, 142
Watermelon Slices 94
Watling, Belle Wicked Mint Julep (see Belle Watling's Wicked Mint Julep)
Whipped Potato Cups 138, 144
Wild Rice 150, 152
Wilkes, John Pit-Roasted Pig (see John Wilkes' Pit-Roasted Pig)

166